FOOD&WINE

BEST OF THE BEST

EDITOR IN CHIEF **Dana Cowin**
EXECUTIVE EDITOR **Kate Heddings**
EDITOR **Susan Choung**
RECIPE TESTER **Ben Mims**
WINE EDITOR **Megan Krigbaum**
COPY EDITOR **Lisa Leventer**
EDITORIAL ASSISTANT **Manon Cooper**
CONTRIBUTING WRITERS **Julia Heffelfinger,**
   Ben Mims, Chelsea Morse, Annie P. Quigley,
   M. Elizabeth Sheldon
RESEARCHER **CB Owens**

DESIGNER **Phoebe Flynn Rich**
PRODUCTION DIRECTOR **Joseph Colucci**
PRODUCTION MANAGER **Stephanie Thompson**
ASSOCIATE PHOTO EDITOR **Samantha Bolton**

FRONT & BACK COVERS
PHOTOGRAPHER **Nicole Franzen**
FOOD STYLIST **Christopher Barsch**
PROP STYLIST **Brooke Deonarine**

Copyright © 2015 Time Inc. Books

Published by Time Inc. Books
1271 Avenue of the Americas • New York, NY 10020

FOOD & WINE is a trademark of Time Inc. Affluent Media
Group, registered in the U.S. and other countries.

ISBN 10: 0-8487-4649-X
ISBN 13: 978-0-8487-4649-0
ISSN 1524-2862

Manufactured in the United States of America

FOOD & WINE

BEST OF THE BEST

The Best Recipes from the 25 Best Cookbooks of the Year

FOOD & WINE
BOOKS

Time Inc. Affluent Media Group, New York

CONTENTS

Recipe titles in **bold** are brand-new dishes appearing exclusively in *Best of the Best.*

continued on next page

CONTENTS *continued*

Recipe titles in **bold** are brand-new dishes appearing exclusively in *Best of the Best*.

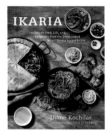

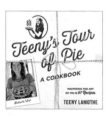

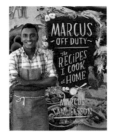
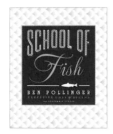

RECIPES

In a *A Good Food Day*, chef Marco Canora tells how foods like non-white-flour pastas made him healthier and happier (p. 24).

FOREWORD

Every year, when we select the most outstanding cookbooks for *Best of the Best,* we notice important trends we're excited to share. The 25 spectacular books we chose point to a few obsessions of the moment:

HEALTHY COOKING The demand for healthy, creative recipes that emphasize pleasure over deprivation is on the rise. Several astonishingly lovely cookbooks are devoted to eating well, among them master baker Alice Medrich's *Flavor Flours* and chef Marco Canora's *A Good Food Day,* a celebration of good fats, wholesome pastas and great grains.

FRENCH FOOD REVIVAL Bordeaux blogger Mimi Thorisson shares classic French recipes in her dreamy but startlingly easy cookbook *A Kitchen in France,* while expat David Lebovitz invites readers to see what's on his stove in *My Paris Kitchen.* Coq au vin is definitely back!

STAR-CHEF TUTORIALS Star chefs are helping home cooks master the basics. With *Inside the Test Kitchen,* Tyler Florence shares the best recipes for everyday classics like pancakes. Geoffrey Zakarian, author of *My Perfect Pantry,* shows how to stock your kitchen shelves with the fundamentals for creative, no-fuss dishes.

We hope you'll use *Best of the Best* not only to get a taste of the biggest trends but also to find your favorite new recipes, knowing that every single one of them is guaranteed to work by the FOOD & WINE Test Kitchen.

Editor in Chief
FOOD & WINE

Executive Editor
FOOD & WINE Cookbooks

Mario Batali, here at Glynwood Farm in Cold Spring, New York, asked Michael Symon, José Andrés and other chef friends to name their most trusted farmers.

AMERICA FARM TO TABLE

Simple, Delicious Recipes Celebrating Local Farmers

BY MARIO BATALI AND JIM WEBSTER

Mario Batali hangs out with Bono, but to him, farmers are the real rock stars. This book is the chef's earnest plea to support local growers: It's not just environmentally correct; using the best, freshest ingredients is the home cook's "most important trick" for making restaurant-quality food. Batali asked chefs across the country to introduce their favorite producers, which inspired him to create over 100 rustic, simple recipes. For instance, he makes saltimbocca, chicken wrapped with sage in crispy prosciutto (p. 14), to showcase poultry from Wedge Oak Farm outside Nashville. Farmer Karen Overton allows her birds to roam free, peck at calcium-rich oyster shells and listen to the radio (they're partial to jazz and NPR). These behind-the-scenes glimpses, along with Batali's immensely appealing recipes, make this book more than an "Eat local" manifesto: It's a fun, incredibly informed guide to delicious fresh food.

Published by Grand Central Publishing, $35

CHICKEN SALTIMBOCCA

WEDGE OAK FARM / Nashville
Serves **4**

1 cup all-purpose flour

Kosher salt and freshly ground black pepper

8 boneless, skinless chicken thighs

8 large fresh sage leaves

8 large slices prosciutto

¼ cup extra-virgin olive oil

4 shallots, thinly sliced

1 pound of a mix of cremini and oyster mushrooms, cut into ¼-inch pieces

1 cup sweet marsala wine

½ cup chicken stock

2 tablespoons unsalted butter

1 bunch fresh flat-leaf parsley, finely chopped (¼ cup)

EDITOR'S WINE CHOICE
Focused, earthy Piedmontese red, such as Barolo.

I use boneless, skinless thighs as the base of this recipe, and the prosciutto yields a fine, durable, crisp crust to the final dish. Be sure to cook it until it becomes a nice deep golden brown with an almost leathery texture, which softens slightly in the sweet marsala bath.

Place the flour in a shallow bowl and season with salt and pepper. Lightly pound the chicken thighs to ¼-inch thickness. Season with salt and pepper and lay a sage leaf on each thigh. Lay 1 slice prosciutto over each thigh and fold in half like a book. Secure the two sides with a toothpick and dredge the whole piece in the seasoned flour.

In a 12- to 14-inch sauté pan, heat the oil until just smoking. Add the chicken and sauté until golden brown on both sides, then transfer to a plate. Add the shallots and mushrooms to the pan and cook until the mushrooms have sweated out their liquid, 5 to 6 minutes. Add the marsala and chicken stock and cook over high heat until reduced by half. Return the chicken thighs to the pan with the sauce and simmer for 3 minutes. Swirl in the butter, add the parsley, and serve.

CHICKEN KIEV WITH GOAT CHEESE & CHOPPED GREENS

KINNIKINNICK FARM / Chicago
Serves **6 to 8**

¼ cup extra-virgin olive oil

2 cloves garlic, thinly sliced

1 bunch (½ pound) lacinato kale, cut into ½-inch ribbons

Kosher salt

4 tablespoons (½ stick) unsalted butter, at room temperature

4 ounces soft goat cheese

3 tablespoons fresh tarragon leaves, or 2 teaspoons dried

8 boneless, skin-on chicken thighs, pounded ¼ inch thick by your butcher

Freshly ground black pepper

2½ cups panko bread crumbs

2 large eggs

1 teaspoon whole milk

½ cup all-purpose flour

1 quart virgin olive oil

This is an adaptation of my dear mother-in-law Lillian Cahn's take on the Russian classic. She added the goat cheese and I added the tarragon and kale. It would have made her very happy to see this, may she rest in peace. She was a glorious spirit and radiates light to this day.

In a 12-inch sauté pan, heat the ¼ cup of oil over medium heat. Add the garlic and sauté until light brown, about 1 minute, then add the kale and 1 teaspoon salt and cook, stirring regularly, until the kale is fully cooked, gray–olive green, and very tender, 10 to 12 minutes. Remove and allow to cool completely. Place the cooled kale in a food processor, add the butter, goat cheese, and tarragon, and process until smooth. Transfer to a bowl and chill for 30 minutes.

Lay eight 10-inch-long pieces of plastic wrap on the counter, separately. Lay 1 chicken thigh on each piece of plastic wrap, season with salt and pepper, and place 1½ tablespoons of the kale-butter and 1 tablespoon of the panko in the center of each piece. Using the plastic wrap to assist, fold in the ends of the thigh and roll, completely enclosing the kale-butter mixture. Roll very tightly in the plastic to create an impermeable log. Keep in mind that any loose edge will allow the kale mixture to leak out, so be very attentive. Repeat with each thigh. Place the wrapped thighs in the refrigerator for 2 hours, or up to overnight.

Place the eggs and milk in a flat bowl and whisk to combine. Place the flour and a pinch of salt and pepper in another flat bowl. Place the remaining 2 cups panko in a third bowl with 2 tablespoons salt.

Heat 2 inches of oil in a Dutch oven or a high-sided sauté pan over medium-high heat until it registers 375°F on a deep-fry thermometer.

Remove the chicken from the plastic wrap. Dip each thigh into the flour mixture, shaking off any excess. Dip the thighs into the egg mixture, letting any excess drip off, then roll in the panko. Gently place each thigh in the hot oil, sealed side down, and cook until golden brown, 6 to 8 minutes on each side, until the internal temperature registers 165°F on a meat thermometer. Transfer to a wire rack set on a rimmed baking sheet and allow to drain for a minute before serving. If not serving immediately, you can hold the chicken in a preheated 300°F oven for up to 30 minutes.

EDITOR'S WINE CHOICE
Vibrant, lightly oaked, full-bodied Chardonnay.

CREAMY KALE GRATIN

KINNIKINNICK FARM / Chicago
Serves **6 to 8**

- 2 tablespoons kosher salt, plus more as needed
- 6 tablespoons (¾ stick) unsalted butter, plus more for the baking dish
- ½ cup chopped Spanish or white onion
- 2 whole cloves
- ¼ cup all-purpose flour
- 2 cups whole milk
- 3 bunches kale (about 1½ pounds), roughly chopped
- ½ cup plus 2 tablespoons grated Parmigiano-Reggiano
- ½ teaspoon freshly grated nutmeg
- Freshly ground black pepper

This dish is the best of steakhouse-style creamed spinach with a rich mineral backbone that makes it work even better with big steak and red wine. If you want to jack it up a bit, add some bacon to the onion when you are cooking it for the béchamel.

Bring 8 quarts water to a boil and add 2 tablespoons salt. Set up an ice bath in a large bowl.

Preheat the oven to 375°F. Butter a 9-inch round gratin dish.

In a heavy-bottomed, medium saucepan, melt the butter over medium heat. Add the onion and cloves and cook until golden brown, about 10 minutes.

Add the flour and stir until light golden brown, about 7 minutes.

Gradually whisk in the milk and cook until the mixture boils and thickens, about 10 minutes.

Reduce the heat to low and simmer, whisking frequently, for 5 minutes more. Remove the cloves.

Add the kale to the boiling water and cook until just wilted and tender, about 2 minutes. Drain the kale and transfer to the ice bath to cool for 5 minutes, then drain well.

Roll up the cooked kale in a kitchen towel or cheesecloth and squeeze out as much liquid as possible.

Finely chop the cooked kale, then add it to the warm sauce. Add ½ cup of the Parmigiano and the nutmeg, season with salt and pepper, and mix well.

Pour the mixture into the buttered gratin dish, top with the remaining 2 tablespoons Parmigiano, and bake for 30 minutes, until bubbly.

CAPONATA "SUBS"

REFUGEE RESPONSE / Cleveland
Serves **4**

- ¼ cup extra-virgin olive oil, plus more as needed
- 2 cloves garlic, halved
- 1 large Spanish onion, cut into ½-inch dice
- 2 ribs celery, cut into thin ¼-inch slices
- 2 teaspoons chopped fresh thyme
- 2 medium eggplant, cut into ½-inch cubes (about 4 cups)
- Kosher salt
- One 6-ounce can tomato paste
- ¼ cup dried currants
- ¼ cup pine nuts
- 1 teaspoon ground cinnamon
- 1 teaspoon unsweetened cocoa powder
- 1 tablespoon red pepper flakes
- 2 tablespoons red wine vinegar
- 2 teaspoons sugar
- Freshly ground black pepper
- ¼ cup water
- 1 baguette, cut into 4 pieces, split open to stuff
- ¼ cup freshly grated Pecorino Romano
- ¼ pound provolone, grated

EDITOR'S WINE CHOICE
Juicy, medium-bodied Italian red, such as Montepulciano.

I have eaten many eggplant Parmigiana over the years in New Jersey and in Little Italy, but this caponata variation is easier, lighter, more delicious, and just plain less messy to make. Unused caponata becomes tomorrow's lunch or tonight's antipasto in a flash.

Preheat the oven to 375°F.

In a 12- to 14-inch sauté pan, heat the olive oil over medium-high heat until almost smoking. Add the garlic, onion, celery, thyme, eggplant, and a couple of pinches of salt. Stir together, reduce the heat to medium, and cook for 5 to 6 minutes, or until the eggplant turns golden. If it looks a little dry, add 1 tablespoon of oil.

Add the tomato paste, currants, pine nuts, cinnamon, cocoa powder, and red pepper flakes and continue to cook for 3 minutes more.

Add the vinegar and allow it to evaporate. Add the sugar, salt and pepper to taste, and water and cook for 5 minutes more, then remove from the heat.

Place the baguette pieces in the oven to toast until golden. Remove and stuff each baguette piece with about ½ cup of the caponata and top with Pecorino Romano and provolone. Place the stuffed bread on a baking sheet and return it to the oven. Bake until the cheese is nicely melted. Remove and serve immediately.

PENNETTE WITH CABBAGE, SPECK & CHESTNUTS

Total **1 hr**; Serves **4**

"The Alto Adige region of northern Italy is often overlooked, but just like in the rest of the 'boot,' the food is tasty, rich and simple," Mario Batali says about this regional pasta. *"If there are any leftovers, I sauté them in a nonstick pan till crisp, almost like spaetzle."*

- 1 cup extra-virgin olive oil
- 1 cup fresh breadcrumbs
- ¼ pound thinly sliced speck, cut crosswise into ¼-inch-wide ribbons
- 7 ounces cooked chestnuts, lightly broken up (1 cup)
- 1 medium white onion, finely chopped
- 3 garlic cloves, smashed and peeled
- ½ medium head of napa cabbage, cut crosswise into ½-inch-wide ribbons
- 6 tablespoons unsalted butter, cut into tablespoons
- Maldon salt or other flaky sea salt and black pepper
- 1 pound pennette
- ¾ cup freshly grated Parmigiano-Reggiano cheese
- 1½ teaspoons finely chopped thyme

EDITOR'S WINE CHOICE
Lively, fruit-forward white from Italy's Alto Adige region.

1. In a small saucepan, bring the olive oil to a simmer with the breadcrumbs. Cook over high heat, stirring, until the breadcrumbs are golden brown and crisp, 3 to 4 minutes. Pour the breadcrumbs and oil through a sieve set over a heatproof bowl. Spread the breadcrumbs on paper towels to drain.

2. Pour ¼ cup of the strained oil into a large saucepan; reserve the rest for another use. Add the speck, chestnuts, onion and garlic to the oil and cook over moderate heat, stirring, until the onion is translucent, 5 minutes. Add the cabbage and cook until softened, 10 minutes. Stir in the butter, season with salt and pepper and remove from the heat.

3. In a large pot of salted boiling water, cook the pennette until al dente. Drain the pasta, reserving ⅓ cup of the cooking water. Stir the pasta and reserved cooking water into the cabbage along with the Parmigiano-Reggiano and thyme. Cook over moderate heat, stirring, for 1 minute. Transfer the pasta to a platter and sprinkle with the toasted breadcrumbs. Serve immediately.

FOR MORE ON MARIO BATALI
mariobatali.com
Mario Batali
@Mariobatali

A GOOD FOOD DAY

Reboot Your Health with Food That Tastes Great

BY MARCO CANORA WITH TAMMY WALKER

Delicious, easy, feel-good dishes like creamed corn made with pureed kernels instead of cream (p. 30) are the focus of Marco Canora's terrific new book chronicling the star chef's return from a host of health problems: sleep apnea, prediabetes, high cholesterol, gout. Canora speaks frankly about the years he spent "overcaffeinated, dehydrated, overstimulated and full of starch, sugar, fatty meat, alcohol and nicotine" even while cooking thoughtfully sourced, rustic Italian food at Hearth in New York City. Here, he's found a way to translate his belief that "deprivation isn't the solution—satisfaction is" into dishes like braised, crisp-skinned chicken thighs with olives (p. 28). And for anyone who points out that chicken breasts are lower in fat than those thighs, he rightfully replies that the dark meat not only tastes better, it's more nutritious.

Published by Clarkson Potter, $30

ESCAROLE SALAD WITH PEAR & PECORINO

Serves **4 to 6**

1 head escarole, washed, cored, leaves torn into bite-size pieces

½ red onion, thinly sliced

1 Bosc pear, thinly sliced or shaved on a mandoline

½ cup toasted walnuts—¼ cup chopped and ¼ cup ground (do this with a coffee grinder)

¼ cup finely grated Pecorino Romano cheese, plus a small chunk for shaving on top

Honey-Cider Vinaigrette (see Editor's Note)

Fine sea salt and freshly ground black pepper

EDITOR'S NOTE

Canora likes to serve this salad with a sweet and tangy vinaigrette that's 1 part honey to 2 parts apple cider vinegar to 4 parts extra-virgin olive oil.

We serve this classic winter salad at Hearth, but I often make it at home too because it comes together fast. Escarole is a sturdy, leafy lettuce that's high in fiber and beta carotene, which the body converts into vitamin A and vitamin K. Slightly bitter escarole and sweet pear are great mates, but what makes this hearty salad really sing is using the walnuts and cheese in two different forms. Finely grated cheese and ground walnuts coat the leaves, so their flavors permeate the whole salad. Shavings of cheese and chopped walnuts allow you to have bigger bursts of those flavors with some crunch. Don't be shy with the pepper here—it goes great with pecorino cheese.

In a large bowl, combine the escarole, onion, pear, ground walnuts, and grated Pecorino. Add as much vinaigrette as you like, along with salt and a generous amount of pepper. Toss to combine. Scatter the chopped walnuts and Pecorino shavings over the top and serve.

BRAISED CHICKEN THIGHS WITH GARLIC, LEMON & GREEK OLIVES

Serves **4**

8 bone-in, skin-on chicken thighs

Fine sea salt and freshly ground black pepper

3 tablespoons extra-virgin olive oil

12 garlic cloves, peeled

2 large yellow onions, thinly sliced (about 4 cups)

1 lemon, thinly sliced and seeds discarded

2 tablespoons fresh oregano leaves, plus more for garnish

1 cup mixed Greek olives

Juice of 1 lemon

AUTHOR'S NOTE

Yes, dark meat has more fat than white meat, but the difference is minimal—about 1 gram per ounce. Dark meat also delivers considerably more iron and B vitamins and twice the amount of zinc as white meat.

The olives provide saltiness here, so go easy on the salt in steps 1 and 3.

EDITOR'S WINE CHOICE

Aromatic, ripe, full-bodied Rhône white.

This easy one-pot dinner is all about chicken thighs, the underdog of the poultry world. The thighs' dark, nutrient-dense meat is undeniably richer, juicier, and more tender than white meat. Also, high demand for boneless, skinless chicken breasts means the deep flavor and juicy potential of the chicken thighs comes at an unbelievable value. Thighs on the bone are a forgiving cut that can take the heat without drying out, so the meat turns out meltingly soft and juicy. The lemon slices cook down in the liquid gold of the chicken fat and juice, infusing the whole dish with bright flavor that balances the richness of the meat. This comes together in about an hour and is simple enough for a weeknight dinner, and fancy enough to serve to guests.

1. Let the chicken come to room temperature about 20 minutes before cooking. Preheat the oven to 350°F. Season the chicken on both sides with salt and pepper.

2. In an ovenproof pan (a 3.5-quart braiser or Dutch oven) large enough to hold all the thighs in a single layer, heat the olive oil over high heat. When the pan is hot and the oil slides easily across the pan, add the thighs skin-side down. Resist the urge to move them around, allowing them to cook untouched until you get a nice, golden brown sear on the skin, 5 to 6 minutes. Add the garlic cloves to the pan and flip each thigh over. Cook until the garlic has taken on some browning, about 3 minutes. Remove the chicken and garlic from the pan and set on a plate.

3. With the pan still over high heat, add the onions, lemon slices, oregano, and salt and pepper to taste. Stir to coat everything in the oil and loosen up the browned bits on the bottom of the pan. Cook for 5 minutes. Nestle the thighs skin-side up in the onion mixture and add the cooked garlic cloves and the olives. Squeeze the lemon juice over the chicken and transfer the pan to the oven to bake for 40 minutes. Scatter fresh oregano leaves over the top and serve.

CREAM-FREE CREAMED CORN

Serves **6**

10 ears white corn, shucked

2 tablespoons extra-virgin olive oil

1 small yellow onion, diced

Fine sea salt and freshly ground black pepper

2 teaspoons roughly chopped fresh basil

AUTHOR'S NOTE

Here's how I remove corn kernels from the cob without them flying around and ending up on the floor: Lay the cob on a cutting board and cut horizontally from the tip to the end, removing about three rows. Rotate the cob so it rests on the flat side and remove three more rows. Continue rotating and cutting until all the kernels are removed.

When it's in season, locally grown sweet corn is as good as gold straight off the cob. But for corn-based comfort food, creamed corn is unbeatable. To max out the corn flavor, skip the heavy cream and use the corn itself to provide creaminess. I puree half the kernels to release their natural sweet starches and use this corn "cream" to thicken a mixture of onions and whole corn kernels. It's incredibly good.

1. Cut the corn kernels from the cobs.

2. In a large high-sided skillet, heat the olive oil over medium heat. Add the onion and salt and pepper to taste. Cook until the onion begins to soften, about 10 minutes. Add the corn kernels, another pinch of salt, and ½ cup water. Cook, stirring occasionally, until the corn is almost tender, about 7 minutes.

3. Transfer half of the corn and onion mixture to a blender and process until smooth. Remove the skillet from the heat and stir in the corn puree. Add the basil and season with salt and pepper to taste.

WHOLE-WHEAT RIGATONI WITH CABBAGE, ONION & PORCINI

Active **45 min**; Total **1 hr**; Serves **4 to 6**

- 1 ounce dried porcini mushrooms (2 cups)
- 1½ cups boiling water
- ¼ cup extra-virgin olive oil
- 1 medium white onion, minced
- 3 garlic cloves, thinly sliced
- 1½ tablespoons finely chopped thyme
- 1½ tablespoons finely chopped sage
- ½ head of green cabbage, cored and thinly sliced crosswise
- Fine sea salt and freshly ground black pepper
- 1 pound whole-wheat rigatoni
- 3 tablespoons freshly grated Parmigiano-Reggiano cheese
- 1 tablespoon unsalted butter
- ¼ cup shredded imported Fontina cheese

EDITOR'S WINE CHOICE
Berry-rich, medium-bodied Pinot Noir.

Marco Canora's healthy eating reboot has helped him change his relationship to pasta. Now he reduces his portion sizes and forgoes simple white pasta in favor of the kind made with complex carbs. Not only is the whole-wheat rigatoni in this vegetarian dish better for you, it's delicious with the hearty flavor of the porcini mushrooms.

1. In a heatproof bowl, soak the porcini in the boiling water for 10 minutes. Finely chop the porcini and reserve the soaking liquid.

2. In a large skillet, combine the olive oil with the onion, garlic, thyme and sage and cook over high heat, stirring, until the onion is translucent, 5 minutes. Stir in the porcini and cabbage, season with salt and pepper and cook until the cabbage is wilted and beginning to brown, 15 minutes. Add the reserved porcini soaking liquid, stopping before you reach the grit. Bring to a boil and remove from the heat.

3. In a large pot of salted boiling water, cook the rigatoni until al dente. Drain the pasta, reserving 2 tablespoons of the cooking water. Return the cabbage to low heat and stir in the pasta and reserved cooking water along with 2 tablespoons of the Parmigiano-Reggiano and the butter. Transfer the pasta to a platter and sprinkle with the Fontina and remaining 1 tablespoon of Parmigiano-Reggiano. Serve immediately.

FOR MORE ON MARCO CANORA
marcocanora.com
Chef Marco Canora
@MarcoCanora

LONE STAR
BREAKFAST TACO,
P. 38

TACOLICIOUS

Festive Recipes for Tacos, Snacks, Cocktails & More

BY SARA DESERAN WITH JOE HARGRAVE, ANTELMO FARIA & MIKE BARROW

I n the San Francisco Bay Area, the craving for tacos "exists on a subconscious level," say Sara Deseran and Joe Hargrave, the owners of four margarita-fueled Tacolicious locations. The outstanding recipes in this cookbook, designed to satisfy that craving, range from classic, crackly-crisp carnitas fried in lard (p. 34) to Texas-style breakfast tacos with bacon and poblano chiles (pictured at left). Even the simplest recipes come with useful tips, such as how to choose the best flour tortillas (look for a glossy sheen and a tiny bit of transparency). The book also goes beyond tacos to encompass versatile dishes like a mix of mango and fresh melon tossed with chile salt (p. 36), which can stand on its own as a snack or add crunch to tacos, salads or sandwiches.

Published by Ten Speed Press, $22

CARNITAS TACO

Makes **about 16 tacos**; Serves **4 to 6**

2½ pounds boneless pork shoulder, cut into 2- to 3-inch cubes

1 cup sliced yellow onion

3 cloves garlic, crushed

3 tablespoons dark brown sugar

1½ tablespoons kosher salt

1½ teaspoons dried Mexican oregano

1 bay leaf

2 tablespoons freshly squeezed orange juice

2 teaspoons freshly squeezed lemon juice

½ cup lard

3 tablespoons vegetable oil

Corn tortillas, warmed, for serving

Chopped white onion, chopped fresh cilantro, salsa of choice, and lime wedges, for serving

If heaven exists, it's likely an all-you-can-eat buffet of pork fried in pork fat. (Remember, you're already dead, so there's no risk of heart attack.) Yes, you could make carnitas *using vegetable oil instead of lard. But as they say, life is short. At the restaurant, we render the lard ourselves—something you can do if you can find extra-fatty pork. But for ready-to-go lard, check out your local butcher shop or Mexican market. Although any salsa will do, our chef Mike Garcia loves* carnitas *with chipotle-tomatillo salsa. He puts it simply: "It's one of my favorite flavor combos ever." For extra porkiness, sprinkle the top with crumbled bits of* chicharrones *(fried pork rinds).*

Put the pork in a nonreactive Dutch oven or other large, heavy pot with a lid. Add the onion, garlic, sugar, salt, oregano, bay leaf, orange juice, and lemon juice and toss to coat the meat evenly. Cover and refrigerate for at least 12 hours or up to 24 hours.

Bring the pork to room temperature. Heat the lard in a small pan over medium heat until it melts, then pour it over the pork. Cover the pot, place over medium-low heat, and cook the pork for about 3 hours, until the pork begins to pull apart easily when tested with a fork.

Remove from the heat. Using a slotted spoon, transfer the pork to a bowl. Discard the cooking liquid and clean the pot. Using a couple of forks, shred the pork a bit but not completely, removing any large chunks of fat.

Return the pot to the stove top over high heat and add the oil. At the minute the oil begins to smoke, using tongs or a spoon and working in batches to avoid crowding, carefully add some of the meat to the hot oil and cook, turning as needed, for about 4 minutes, until crisp on all sides. (If some onions are still attached, don't worry about it.)

Serve with the tortillas, onion, cilantro, salsa, and lime.

EDITOR'S NOTE
Look for a fatty pork shoulder for the juiciest carnitas.

EDITOR'S BEER CHOICE
Crisp, lightly hoppy beer, such as pilsner.

MELON, MANGO & CUCUMBER WITH CHILE, SALT & LIME

Serves **4 to 6**

1 small, ripe melon (such as cantaloupe, seedless watermelon, or honeydew), chilled

2 ripe Kent or other large mangoes, or 3 ripe Manila or other small mangoes

1 English cucumber, chilled

2 tablespoons kosher salt

2 tablespoons chile powder of your choice

2 or 3 limes, halved

One of the hallmarks of Mexican cuisine is the flavor combination of salty, spicy, sour, and sweet. It extends from sweets and candies to fresh fruit. In the streets, vendors sell bags of sliced fruit and cucumbers topped with salt, chile powder, and a big squeeze of lemon or lime juice. The following instructions are so simple that they barely qualify as a recipe. Success here is all about finding the best fruit available. Look for Kent mangoes. Big and green, they slice open to reveal the sweetest, most ambrosial flesh. For another presentation, try doing as the street vendors do and slice your fruit and cucumber into spears (pictured) rather than cubes. Serve the spears plunked upright into tall glasses, so people can pick them up with their fingers.

To prepare the melon, cut it in half. If it has a seed cavity, scoop out and discard the seeds. Cut the rind away from the flesh, and then cut the flesh into 1-inch cubes.

To prepare the mangoes, hold a mango on one of its narrow edges, with the stem facing you. Position a sharp knife just to the right of the stem end (or to the left of it if left-handed) and cut downward, running your knife as closely as possible to the pit. Repeat on the opposite side of the pit. Using a paring knife, peel away the skin from each mango "cheek," then slice the flesh into 1-inch cubes.

To prepare the cucumber, cut it in half lengthwise, then cut each half lengthwise in half again. Cut crosswise into 1-inch cubes.

Put the cubed melon, mango, and cucumber in a large bowl, sprinkle with the salt and chile powder, and toss to coat evenly. Taste and adjust with more salt or chile powder if needed.

Serve in little bowls with the lime halves for squeezing in juice as desired.

LONE STAR BREAKFAST TACO

Makes **6 filling tacos;** Serves **6**

2 **small poblano chile peppers**

3 **slices thick-cut bacon, cut into 1-inch pieces**

5 **small new potatoes (about 8 ounces total), cut into ¼-inch cubes**

¾ **cup chopped yellow onion**

6 **eggs, whisked**

1 **cup shredded Monterey Jack cheese**

Kosher salt

6 **small flour tortillas**

Chopped fresh cilantro and hot sauce, for serving

Our hometown of San Francisco doesn't seem to share Austin's affinity for the breakfast taco, but it's something every city should get on board with. Pledging allegiance to Texas, we serve these in flour tortillas, but corn tortillas would be equally good. Be sure to place a salsa picante *like Tapatío or, as a nod to the South, the more vinegary Tabasco at the table.*

Place the poblano chiles directly over the flame of a gas burner and turn with tongs for about 3 minutes, until charred and blistered all over. Alternatively, place the chiles in a dry, heavy skillet over high heat and turn with tongs for about 3 minutes, until charred and blistered all over. Transfer the chiles to a bowl, cover with plastic wrap, and let steam for 10 minutes. Remove the chiles and gently peel or scrape away the skin. Slice each chile in half lengthwise, remove the stem and seeds, and cut into strips 1 inch long by ⅛ inch wide. Measure out ⅓ cup. Set the rest aside for another day.

Put the bacon in a large, heavy skillet over medium heat and leave to cook for a few minutes, until some of the fat has rendered. Using a slotted spoon, transfer the bacon to a plate. Add the potatoes to the pan and cook, stirring occasionally, for about 10 minutes, until cooked through. Add the onion and return the bacon to the pan. Cook, stirring occasionally, for another few minutes, until the bacon is cooked and the onion is soft.

Turn down the heat to low. Add the eggs, chiles, and cheese and stir for a few minutes until the eggs are gently scrambled (taking care not to overcook) and the cheese is melted. Season with salt. Remove from the heat.

One at a time, warm the flour tortillas directly over the low flame of a gas burner for 10 to 15 seconds on each side, until puffed. Alternatively, warm them in a heavy, dry skillet over low heat on both sides for about the same amount of time. Serve the eggs with the tortillas, cilantro, and hot sauce.

FLOUR TORTILLAS: THE GOOD, THE BAD, THE UGLY
There are flour tortillas (more often than not puffy, dry, and, for lack of a better description, floury), and then there are flour tortillas. *Any flour tortilla that deserves to be italicized will have a glossy sheen and an almost buttery aroma, appear a tiny bit transparent, and become almost flaky when heated.*

SOPA DE LIMA WITH CORN SALSA

Total **45 min;** Serves **6**

- 1½ cups fresh corn kernels (from 2 ears)
- 1½ cups diced tomato (1 large)
- ½ cup chopped cilantro
- ½ cup finely chopped red onion
- 1 tablespoon finely chopped seeded jalapeño
- ¼ cup fresh lime juice, plus lime wedges for serving
- Kosher salt and pepper
- 2 quarts homemade chicken stock or low-sodium broth
- 2 pounds skinless, boneless chicken thighs
- 1 teaspoon dried Mexican oregano
- Steamed white rice, crumbled queso fresco and diced avocado, for serving

This recipe is a hybrid of a Yucatán-style lime soup and a Oaxacan chicken soup. "It's incredibly simple if you don't make your own broth," Sara Deseran says. "But then again, a soup is only as good as its broth." At Tacolicious, she uses homemade chicken stock.

1. In a medium bowl, toss the corn with the tomato, cilantro, onion, jalapeño and 1 tablespoon of the lime juice. Season the corn salsa with salt and pepper and let stand for about 20 minutes.

2. Meanwhile, in a large pot, bring the stock to a boil. Add the chicken thighs and simmer over moderate heat until cooked through, about 15 minutes. Transfer the chicken to a bowl and let cool. Shred the chicken.

3. Add the oregano and remaining 3 tablespoons of lime juice to the soup and stir in the chicken. Season with salt and pepper. Ladle the soup over rice and garnish with the corn salsa, queso fresco and avocado. Serve with lime wedges.

FOR MORE ON SARA DESERAN

tacolicious.com
Tacolicious
@tacolicious

Maria Elia spent a summer in Cyprus cooking with her father (below); the experience inspired her to write *Smashing Plates*.

SMASHING PLATES

Greek Flavors Redefined

BY MARIA ELIA

After working at renowned restaurants in London and legendary places like El Bulli and Arzak in Spain, British chef Maria Elia took a break to spend a summer cooking at her father's taverna in his native Cyprus—an experience that also involved foraging for caper leaves and hunting game birds. Her passion for the food is clear in this wonderful collection of 140 recipes that explore authentic Greek flavors, like the briny grape leaves she adds to chicken and orzo soup (p. 44). Whether explaining the Greek reverence for olive oil ("It's used to mark the sign of the cross at a child's baptism") or the nuances of feta ("barrel-matured is the tastiest"), Elia expresses a heartfelt nostalgia for the cuisine even while she reinvents it.

Published by Kyle Books, $28

CARROT KEFTEDES

Serves **4 (makes 16)**

12 oz carrots, trimmed and peeled but left whole

2 tablespoons olive oil

1 small onion, grated

1 cup feta, crumbled

½ cup fresh bread crumbs

1 teaspoon cinnamon

2 teaspoons dried mint

½ cup grated Parmesan or Kefalotyri

¼ cup finely chopped fresh flat-leaf parsley

1 free-range egg, beaten

Sea salt and freshly ground black pepper

All-purpose flour, to dust

Olive or vegetable oil, for frying

EDITOR'S WINE CHOICE
Vibrant, fruit-forward sparkling wine, such as Spanish cava.

Normally, keftedes are made with ground meat (they're basically meatballs). These vegetarian alternatives are packed with flavor. Pre-roasting the carrots brings out their natural sweetness which is balanced by the salty, sour feta and Kefalotyri. Mint and parsley add freshness, with a hint of cinnamon for spice. Serve with Pomegranate Skordalia and Carrot Tabbouleh. These keftedes are just as delicious served cold.

Preheat the oven to 400°F.

Place the carrots in a roasting pan. Drizzle with the olive oil and cook for 30 to 40 minutes (depending on the size of carrots) until al dente, turning them halfway through. Let cool.

Grate the carrots into a bowl and mix with the rest of the ingredients, except the flour and oil. Season with salt and pepper and refrigerate for an hour to firm up. (The mixture can be made the day before and refrigerated until required.)

Shape into 16 walnut-sized balls, then flatten into patties and dust with flour. You can either shallow-fry them in olive oil or deep-fry them in vegetable oil. If using olive oil, heat in a frying pan over medium heat, add half the keftedes, and cook until golden on either side—about 3 minutes. Repeat with the remaining balls. If using vegetable oil, deep-fry for about 3 minutes at 350°F until golden. Drain on paper towels and serve warm with the suggested accompaniments.

CHICKEN SOUP WITH ORZO, SHREDDED GRAPE LEAVES, TOMATOES, LEMON & HERBS

Serves **4 to 6**

2 tablespoons olive oil

1 onion, finely diced

2 garlic cloves, finely chopped

A pinch of ground allspice

1 teaspoon ground cinnamon

1 quart chicken stock

¾ cup orzo

4 large, vine-ripened tomatoes, peeled and diced

8 grape leaves (fresh or pickled), trimmed of stem and shredded (see Note)

2 cups shredded cooked chicken

¼ cup finely chopped fresh mint

¼ cup finely chopped fresh dill

¼ cup finely chopped fresh flat-leaf parsley

2 tablespoons freshly squeezed lemon juice

Sea salt and freshly ground black pepper

Extra-virgin olive oil, to serve

There's nothing more comforting than a bowl of chicken soup… I'd recommend you poach a whole chicken a day in advance. Or, if you have half a roast chicken left over, strip the meat from it and make a stock from the roasted carcass: place the stripped carcass in a pot with ½ an onion, 2 cloves garlic, 1 rib celery, a bay leaf, and a carrot if you have one. Cover with cold water and place over low heat for 1 hour. Turn off heat and let cool before straining. Discard the carcass and aromatics, and your stock is ready!

I adore the flavor and smell of stuffed grape leaves. They bring back childhood memories of spending Sundays at my Aunty Stella's, and to this day I've never eaten a dolmades (stuffed grape leaves) as good as hers.

While writing this recipe I got to thinking that some soaked raisins and shaved Kefalotyri would be good to serve with this soup. I also tried it topped with a little crumbled feta, which was great. Next time I make it I'm going to add some peeled fava beans. Basically, go with whatever you think sounds good!

Heat the oil in a medium saucepan over medium heat, add the onion, and cook for 5 to 8 minutes, until softened and transparent.

Add the garlic, allspice, and cinnamon and cook for another minute, then add the chicken stock and bring almost to a boil. Add the orzo, tomatoes, grape leaves, and chicken, then reduce the heat so the soup is simmering. Cook for approximately 8 minutes, or until the orzo is tender.

Add the fresh herbs and lemon juice and season with salt and pepper. Serve drizzled with extra-virgin olive oil.

NOTE

If using fresh grape leaves, blanch them in boiling salted water for about 2 minutes until they're no longer bright green; refresh under cold running water. If using pickled or jarred leaves, place in a colander and rinse well.

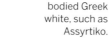

EDITOR'S WINE CHOICE
Citrusy, medium-bodied Greek white, such as Assyrtiko.

ZUCCHINI, CAPER & HERB LINGUINE

Serves **4 to 6**

2 medium zucchini, trimmed

10½ oz fresh linguine (dried is fine if it's all you have)

A good glug of olive oil

¼ cup plus 2 tablespoons salted capers, rinsed and dried

2 garlic cloves, finely chopped

A pinch of dried red pepper flakes (optional)

½ cup chopped mint

¾ cup chopped fresh dill

¼ cup chopped fresh flat-leaf parsley

Sea salt and freshly ground black pepper

7 tablespoons butter, diced

1¼ cups freshly grated Kefalotyri, Parmesan, or Pecorino

EDITOR'S WINE CHOICE
Zesty, slightly herbal New Zealand Sauvignon Blanc.

We didn't tend to eat a lot of pasta at home when I was a child as my mother is a diabetic, but I remember my dad serving spaghetti with steak in his restaurant, and it was always a real treat. I spent nine months working in Tuscany several years ago, and that totally sorted my pasta cravings out! This recipe is full of fresh flavors and takes no time to make. For an even quicker option, you can cook the zucchini with the pasta (just add 4 minutes before the end).

Slice the zucchini lengthwise as thinly as possible and cut into long shreds.

Cook the pasta in boiling, salted water according to the package instructions, then drain in a colander, reserving a little of the cooking water.

While the pasta is cooking, heat the olive oil in a large frying pan over medium heat, add the capers, and cook until crisp. Set aside, heat a little more oil in the pan, and cook the zucchini, garlic, and pepper flakes, if using, until they are just tender. (You may need to cook the zucchini in two batches depending on the size of your pan.)

Toss the zucchini with the drained pasta, along with the capers and herbs. Season with salt and pepper. Add the butter, ¼ cup of the reserved cooking water, and half the cheese and mix well. Serve immediately, sprinkled with the remaining cheese.

VARIATION

A lovely variation to this recipe is to cook some peeled shrimp with the capers and then add a little freshly grated lemon zest at the end.

SESAME BUNS

Makes **8 rolls—perhaps more than you'll need, but who can resist freshly baked bread?!**

¼ oz active dried yeast

2 teaspoons superfine sugar

½ cup warm water

¾ cup warm milk

4 cups all-purpose flour, plus extra for dusting

1 tablespoon butter, diced

1 teaspoon ground allspice

2 teaspoons ground cinnamon

2 teaspoons salt

Olive oil, for greasing

1 free-range egg, beaten

Sesame seeds, for sprinkling

Try these topped with sun-ripened tomatoes, fresh basil, and a drizzle of olive oil and sea salt. I have also used them with Pulled Lamb Burgers and Fava Bean and Mint Hummus. If you prefer to make a loaf, you'll need to extend the cooking time by about 10 minutes.

Mix the yeast, sugar, water, and milk together until the yeast dissolves and let ferment for about 10 minutes.

Sift the flour into a large mixing bowl and rub in the butter until it resembles bread crumbs. Combine with the allspice, cinnamon, and salt (or flavoring of choice). Make a well in the center and pour in the yeast mix. Combine all the ingredients together to form a sticky dough. Turn onto a lightly floured surface and knead until it becomes smooth and elastic, about 20 minutes. This is good for the biceps—alternatively, use the dough hook attachment of an electric mixer. (If you want to add some olives or cheese, now's the time to add and knead them in.) Put the dough in a lightly oiled bowl, cover, and leave in a warm place until doubled in size, about 1 to 1½ hours.

Turn the dough onto the floured work surface again, punch down to knock out the air, then divide it into 8 pieces and shape them into balls. Use the palm of your hand or a rolling pin to flatten a little. Place on a lightly oiled baking sheet, cover, and set aside to rise for another hour in a warm place until doubled in size. Meanwhile, preheat the oven to 425°F.

Brush the rolls with egg, sprinkle with sesame seeds, and bake for about 10 minutes until they are golden and sound hollow when their bottoms are tapped. Cool slightly on a wire rack and serve warm.

VARIATIONS

Add 2¼ tablespoons chopped Kalamata olives or ¾ cup crumbled feta cheese. You may want to try sprinkling with a little dried oregano, mint, or sumac or anise, cumin, or fennel seeds. Alternatively, add a little finely grated lemon zest.

GREEK PULLED-DUCK BURGERS

Active **1 hr 15 min**; Total **5 hr 15 min plus 8 hr brining**; Serves **6**

BRINED DUCK

- **1 cup fine sea salt**
- **⅓ cup packed light brown sugar**
- **¼ cup sherry vinegar**
- **⅔ cup fresh orange juice, plus 6 strips of orange zest**
- **1 head of garlic, halved crosswise**
- **2 teaspoons fennel seeds**
- **One 3-inch cinnamon stick**
- **Pinch of crushed red pepper**
- **6 duck legs (4½ pounds total)**

PULLED DUCK

- **2 small yellow onions, halved and thinly sliced**
- **4 garlic cloves**
- **½ cup fresh orange juice, plus 2 strips of orange zest**
- **2 tablespoons fennel seeds**
- **1 tablespoon ground coriander**
- **1 tablespoon cumin seeds**
- **Pinch of crushed red pepper**
- **2 bay leaves, crumbled**

TO SERVE

- **6 brioche burger buns, split**
- **1 dill pickle, thinly sliced**
- **1 bunch of watercress, thick stems discarded**
- **Celery Root & Apple Slaw (recipe follows)**

EDITOR'S WINE CHOICE
Fragrant, red-berried Greek red, such as Agiorgitiko.

Maria Elia gives duck legs the pulled-pork treatment: She slow-roasts them until they're falling-apart tender, then tosses the shredded meat in the flavorful juices. She likes to have the duck in sandwiches with spiced duck popcorn (popped in duck fat) and celery root slaw while watching one of her favorite American TV shows: Duck Dynasty, her inspiration for this recipe.

1. Brine the duck In a large pot, whisk the salt, sugar and vinegar with 4 cups of water to dissolve the salt and sugar. Stir in the orange juice and zest, garlic, fennel seeds, cinnamon stick and crushed red pepper. Bring to a simmer and remove from the heat. Stir in 8 cups of cold water. Transfer the brine to a container large enough to hold the duck and let cool completely. Add the duck legs and cover with an upside-down plate to keep them submerged. Refrigerate for at least 8 hours or overnight.

2. Make the pulled duck Preheat the oven to 400°F. Remove the duck and cinnamon stick from the brine. Discard the brine and pat the duck dry. In a roasting pan, toss the onions with the garlic, orange juice and zest and the cinnamon stick. In a small bowl, mix the fennel seeds, coriander, cumin, crushed red pepper and bay leaves. Rub the spices all over the duck legs and set them on top of the onions, skin side up. Add 6 cups of water to the pan and roast for 20 minutes. Baste the legs, then reduce the oven temperature to 325°F and roast until the duck is tender and pulls away easily from the bones, 2 to 2½ hours.

3. Transfer the duck legs to a plate and let cool. Discard the cinnamon stick and orange zest. Transfer the cooking liquid and onions to a medium saucepan and skim off the fat. Bring to a boil over moderately high heat, then reduce the heat to moderate and simmer until reduced to ⅔ cup, about 1½ hours.

4. Serve the burgers Shred the duck legs. Discard the skin and bones. In a large bowl, mix the duck meat with the reduced sauce. Mound the duck on the brioche buns and top with the pickle, watercress and Celery Root & Apple Slaw.

Celery Root & Apple Slaw

Active **20 min;** Total **1 hr 20 min;** Serves **6**

In a medium bowl, mix the celery root, apple, mayonnaise, lemon juice and mustard. Season with salt and pepper. Cover and refrigerate for at least 1 hour before serving.

- 1 small celery root, peeled and coarsely grated (about 3 cups)
- 1 Granny Smith apple, grated (about 1 cup)
- ½ cup mayonnaise
- 2 tablespoons fresh lemon juice
- 1 tablespoon whole-grain mustard

  Kosher salt and pepper

FOR MORE ON MARIA ELIA
thisismariaelia.com
🐦 @thisismariaelia

Tyler Florence photographed the recipes for his book with an iPad, sharing images as he was testing.

INSIDE THE TEST KITCHEN

120 New Recipes, Perfected

BY TYLER FLORENCE

When Food Network star Tyler Florence asked his social media followers what they wanted to learn how to cook, he was surprised by the number of requests for basics like pancakes. "Obviously, recipes for pancakes already exist (I should know; I've written a few of them)," he says. But "there was a missing link, something people weren't getting." So he and his test kitchen crew worked "to make each recipe the best possible, in the most time-efficient way." He shares the results in this collection of luxurious comfort-food classics, along with tricks and tips: A splash of water is the key to making a wonderfully creamy Caesar dressing (p. 56), for example; then, any leftover dressing can be used to punch up deviled egg filling. And not only did he perfect those pancakes (cornstarch keeps them fluffy and tender), but the recipe also serves as an easy base for waffles, muffins, cookies and more.

Published by Clarkson Potter, $35

HERB-ROASTED WILD MUSHROOMS WITH RED WINE & CREAM

RECIPE NO. 114
Serves **4 to 6**

2 pounds assorted mushrooms
(such as cremini, oyster,
shiitake, chanterelle, black
trumpet)

Extra-virgin olive oil

6 bay leaves

4 thyme sprigs

2 rosemary sprigs, cut into
1-inch pieces

3 shallots, 2 cut in half

Kosher salt

Freshly ground black pepper

1 tablespoon unsalted butter

1 teaspoon whole peppercorns

2 cups good red wine

¼ cup heavy cream

¼ cup arugula leaves

**EDITOR'S
WINE CHOICE**
Bold,
concentrated
California
Chardonnay.

We're lucky to have great wild mushrooms in northern California in the fall. Roasting the mushrooms caramelizes their edges, creating nice textures and deep flavors, while the wine and cream sauce brings both acidity and richness. You can serve this side dish with everything from Super-Crisp Roast Chicken to Seared Brined Pork Chops and salmon.

Preheat the oven to 450°F. Brush the mushrooms clean of any dirt and trim off any deep blemishes. Slice about ¼ inch thick. Put the mushrooms in one layer on one or more sheet pans (as necessary), and drizzle with a little olive oil. Add 4 bay leaves, the thyme and rosemary sprigs, and the 2 halved shallots. Season generously with salt and pepper. Roast about 15 minutes, until the mushrooms caramelize and are golden brown.

Slice the remaining shallot into rings and break the rings apart with your hands. Heat a small saucepan with the butter over medium heat. Add the shallot, 2 remaining bay leaves, the peppercorns, and 1 tablespoon olive oil. Cook the shallot, stirring, until a deep caramel brown. Add the wine and let the mixture reduce until it coats the back of a spoon, about 10 minutes. Add the cream and cook until it thickens again, about 2 minutes more. Season with salt to taste.

Transfer the roasted mushrooms to a serving dish, removing the bay leaves and herb stems, and drizzle with the sauce. Garnish with the arugula.

CAESAR DRESSING

Makes **about 2 cups**

6 **anchovy fillets**

5 **garlic cloves**

1 **whole egg plus 2 yolks**

Juice of 1 lemon

1 **tablespoon Dijon mustard**

1 **cup grapeseed or canola oil**

1 **tablespoon extra-virgin olive oil**

¼ **cup grated Parmesan cheese**

Sea or kosher salt

Freshly ground black pepper

Place the anchovies, garlic cloves, the egg and yolks, lemon juice, mustard, and a splash of water in a blender and mix. With the blender running, slowly pour in the grapeseed oil to make a thick dressing. Add the olive oil, Parmesan cheese, and salt and pepper to taste, and blend. Refrigerate the dressing if you will not be using it right away.

NOTE

Use leftover dressing in the Caesar Salad "Deviled Eggs."
[See Editor's Note.]

EDITOR'S NOTE

Florence folds leftover dressing into a deviled egg filling. He pipes the filling into small romaine spears, then tops them with white anchovies, anchovy breadcrumbs and grated egg white.

SPAGHETTI WITH SUMMER SQUASH & PINE NUTS

RECIPE NO. 073
Serves **4**

1 large onion

2 medium yellow summer squash

2 medium pattypan squash

2 medium zucchini

2 garlic cloves

Extra-virgin olive oil

Kosher salt

Freshly ground black pepper

2 tablespoons pine nuts

Grapeseed or vegetable oil, for frying

4 squash blossoms

1 pound fresh spaghetti

Grated Parmesan cheese

6 fresh basil leaves

I'm a big fan of letting produce shine, and living in California has definitely driven that idea home. This sauce relies on pureed summer squash for its fresh taste and color. By reserving some cooked pieces of squash and frying up a few squash blossoms, we highlight the abundance of squash in a few different ways. It's also quick to get the dish onto the dinner table, and this is a perfect use for this beautiful, healthful summer vegetable.

Chop the onion into 1-inch pieces, then cut the summer squash, pattypan squash, and zucchini into ¼-inch rounds. Mince the garlic. Generously coat a medium saucepan with some olive oil and set over medium heat. When the oil shimmers, add the vegetables to the pan with a generous pinch of salt and pepper. Cook, stirring occasionally as the vegetables sweat down. Once they are tender but not falling apart, add three-fourths of the vegetables to a blender and reserve the rest in a bowl in a warm place. Blend the squash until smooth, season with salt and pepper to taste, and return to the saucepan. Keep over low heat so it stays warm.

While the squash is cooking, set a large pot of water to boil over high heat and season it generously with salt.

Toast the pine nuts in a tall saucepan over medium heat until aromatic, then remove and set aside. Heat 2 inches of grapeseed oil in that saucepan to 360°F over medium-high heat. Fry the squash blossoms—two at a time if all four don't fit comfortably in the pan—until golden brown. Drain on a paper towel–lined plate and season with salt and pepper.

Cook the spaghetti in the boiling salted water for about 45 seconds, until al dente. Drain, then drizzle olive oil over the pasta. Toss the cooked spaghetti with the blended squash. Top with Parmesan cheese, a drizzle of olive oil, and salt to taste.

Plate the pasta in a serving dish. Top with the remaining vegetables, fried squash blossoms, and pine nuts. Garnish with torn fresh basil leaves and serve with additional Parmesan cheese.

NOTES
• *Use a variety of squash for this.*
• *Pureed vegetables are a healthy, fast sauce.*

EDITOR'S WINE CHOICE
Zesty, herb-scented Sauvignon Blanc, such as Sancerre.

BEETS, BEANS & WINTER GREENS

Active **40 min;** Total **2 hr 30 min plus overnight soaking**
Serves **4 to 6**

6 ounces dried gigante beans
(1 cup), soaked overnight
and drained

3 small red beets, peeled
and quartered

2 thyme sprigs

1 bay leaf

1 sage leaf

1 garlic clove

Kosher salt

1 tablespoon Dijon mustard

1 tablespoon sherry vinegar

2 teaspoons honey

⅓ cup extra-virgin olive oil

½ cup walnuts

4 ounces red Russian kale,
stems discarded, leaves torn
into bite-size pieces

1 red endive, leaves separated

½ medium head of Treviso or
radicchio, cored, leaves torn
into bite-size pieces

½ head of red leaf lettuce, torn
into bite-size pieces

½ fennel bulb, cored and thinly
sliced, fronds reserved and
chopped

½ cup dried cranberries

½ cup crumbled Pecorino-
Romano cheese

"Cooking the beets with the beans was one of those ideas that we just knew was going to work," Tyler Florence says. That the beans take on a vivid color was a pleasant surprise. Blending some of those beans and beets into the vinaigrette results in a pink dressing that's creamy but dairy-free.

1. In a medium saucepan, combine the drained beans with the beets, thyme, bay leaf, sage, garlic and 5½ cups of water. Add 1 tablespoon of salt and bring to a boil. Reduce the heat to moderately low and simmer until the beans are tender, about 1½ hours. Drain the beans, reserving the cooking liquid. Discard the herbs and garlic.

2. In a blender, combine ⅔ cup of the bean cooking liquid with ⅓ cup of the beans and 1 piece of beet. Add the mustard, vinegar, honey and olive oil and puree until smooth. Pour the dressing through a sieve into a bowl and season with salt. Refrigerate until ready to serve.

3. Preheat the oven to 350°F. Spread the walnuts on a baking sheet and bake for 10 minutes, until toasted. Let cool and coarsely chop.

4. Arrange the kale, endive, Treviso and red leaf lettuce on a platter and top with the remaining cooked beans and beets. Sprinkle with the sliced fennel, toasted walnuts and dried cranberries. Drizzle with some of the dressing and sprinkle with the pecorino and chopped fennel fronds. Serve the remaining dressing on the side.

FOR MORE ON TYLER FLORENCE
tylerflorence.com
🐦 @TylerFlorence

This design was inspired by the butler's kitchen in a Rhode Island mansion.

WOLF

THE KITCHN COOKBOOK

Recipes, Kitchens & Tips to Inspire Your Cooking

BY SARA KATE GILLINGHAM & FAITH DURAND

Viewing dramatic kitchen makeovers, then learning the best recipes to make in those inspiring spaces: These are two reasons people love The Kitchn, the massively popular blog on the design site Apartment Therapy. In their debut book, two of the blog's editors have curated their all-time favorite hits from The Kitchn's 10 years. The 150 recipes are geared to "a curious home cook who cares about food and is working to fit cooking into competing demands on time." There are low-maintenance, one-pot meals like a skillet-roasted chicken with perfectly burnished skin (p. 66) and a pasta casserole with broccoli and Gouda, lightened with cottage cheese and yogurt (p. 64). Gillingham and Durand devote as many pages to strategies for setting up and beautifying your kitchen as they do to recipes: "Once you experience the magic of a truly efficient kitchen, it's our hope that you'll cook in it more often."

Published by Clarkson Potter, $32.50

ROASTED EGGPLANT WITH SMOKED ALMONDS & GOAT CHEESE

Serves **6**

2 large eggplants
(about 2½ pounds)

Kosher salt

½ cup olive oil

2 tablespoons cider vinegar

1 tablespoon honey

1 teaspoon smoked paprika

1 teaspoon ground cumin

4 large garlic cloves, minced

3 tablespoons freshly
squeezed lemon juice
(from about 1 lemon)

1 tablespoon soy sauce

1 cup fresh flat-leaf parsley
leaves, roughly chopped

½ cup smoked or roasted
almonds, roughly chopped

2 ounces goat cheese,
crumbled and divided

¼ cup finely chopped scallions

We have made salads from all sorts of vegetables: fennel, cabbage, potato, sweet potato. But an eggplant salad is more rare, even though the eggplant's tender, unctuous innards seemed like they would go so well with other salad staples. So we stepped up to the challenge and created this dish. We love the natural smokiness of roasted eggplant, so here is a lesson in how to play up that flavor with smoked paprika and smoked almonds, as well as to play off the rich ingredients with sharp acids from lemons and creamy goat cheese. All together these flavors create a "salad" that is one of our all-time favorite vegetable side dishes.

Place a rack in the middle of the oven. Preheat the oven to 400°F. Line a large baking sheet with parchment. Cut the eggplant into 1-inch cubes and place them in a large bowl. Sprinkle the eggplant lightly with kosher salt and set aside while making the marinade.

In a small bowl, whisk together the oil, vinegar, honey, smoked paprika, and cumin. Dab away any extra water that has beaded on the eggplant and toss with the marinade. Stir in the garlic. Spread the eggplant on the prepared baking sheet and slide the sheet into the middle of the oven. Reserve the bowl.

Roast the eggplant for 40 minutes, or until very tender and slightly browned. Stir every 15 minutes and check after 30 minutes to make sure it isn't burning. Remove the eggplant from the oven and let it cool a little while making the dressing.

In the large bowl used for marinating the eggplant, whisk together the lemon juice and soy sauce. Return the roasted eggplant to the bowl and toss with the lemon juice mixture. Fold in the parsley leaves, smoked almonds, and most of the goat cheese, reserving a little.

Spread the finished salad in a serving bowl and sprinkle the reserved goat cheese and scallions on top. Serve immediately, while warm. Leftovers keep well in a covered container in the refrigerator for up to 3 days.

TIP FROM THE KITCHN
Look for smoked almonds in the snack aisle of your grocery store, not with the baking ingredients. If you can't find them, roasted almonds make a fine substitute.

PASTA CASSEROLE WITH BROCCOLI & GOUDA CHEESE

Serves **6**

Olive oil

Kosher salt

1 pound dried orecchiette or medium shell pasta

1 small head fresh broccoli (about 1½ pounds), stalk removed, florets reserved

½ cup chopped fresh flat-leaf parsley leaves

2 large shallots, finely chopped (about ¼ cup)

15 ounces small-curd cottage cheese

1 cup plain whole-milk or low-fat yogurt

1 large egg, beaten

1½ teaspoons salt

Freshly ground black pepper

4 ounces aged Gouda cheese, grated (about 1 cup)

EDITOR'S WINE CHOICE
Crisp, pear- and citrus-inflected white, such as Arneis from Italy's Piedmont.

Pasta casseroles are usually a guilty pleasure, packed with cream and three kinds of cheese. But we prefer a lighter pasta bake, one that puts fresh ingredients forward yet lends itself to weeknight convenience. This is one of the quickest casseroles we know. This dish bakes up bubbly and comforting, but at the same time it gives you your daily serving of vegetables, too.

Heat the oven to 350°F and lightly grease a 9 x 13-inch baking dish with olive oil. Fill a large pot three-quarters full with water, salt it generously, and bring to a boil. Add the pasta and cook until al dente, or according to package directions. Drain, return to the cooking pot, and set aside.

Fold the broccoli florets into the pasta, along with the parsley and shallots.

In a separate bowl whisk together the cottage cheese, yogurt, egg, and salt. Fold this mixture into the pasta and season generously with black pepper. Fold in three-quarters of the Gouda cheese.

Spread the casserole ingredients into the prepared baking dish. Sprinkle the top with the remaining cheese. Drizzle lightly with olive oil. (At this point the casserole may be covered and refrigerated for up to 24 hours. Let it come to room temperature before baking it.) Bake for 30 to 35 minutes, or until the cheese on top has melted and the pasta is lightly golden. Serve immediately.

SKILLET-ROASTED WHOLE CHICKEN

Serves **4**

1 tablespoon coarse salt

1 teaspoon freshly ground black pepper

Zest of 1 lemon

1 tablespoon (packed) dark brown sugar

One 3- to 4-pound fresh whole chicken

Olive oil or butter

Lemon halves, garlic cloves, fresh herbs (such as thyme, rosemary, or sage), for stuffing the cavity of the bird (optional)

All of us at The Kitchn adore this method for making a roasted chicken; we borrow it from the much-missed chef Judy Rodgers of Zuni Café in San Francisco. The important things to note are to use a hot skillet, cast iron if possible, and to start with a very dry bird. Have paper towels at the ready to pat her down like a baby coming out of a pool. A small chicken takes only about an hour to cook, so we can easily make this chicken for weeknight meals. Prep it the night before, put it in the oven when you get home from work, and let it cook while you wind down from the day. It's that simple.

Place a 10- to 12-inch skillet, preferably cast iron, on the middle rack of the oven and heat it to 475°F.

In a small bowl, mix the salt, pepper, lemon zest, and brown sugar. Set aside.

Remove any packaging from the chicken and drain out any juices or blood trapped in the plastic. Reach inside the chicken's body cavity and remove the bag of giblets. The giblets can be discarded, saved for stock, or used to make gravy later on.

Pat the chicken very thoroughly with paper towels or a kitchen rag, making sure to absorb any liquid behind the wings or legs and inside the body cavity, too.

Massage the outside of the chicken with olive oil or butter, and then coat it with the spice rub. If desired, stuff the inside of the chicken with halved lemons, whole cloves of garlic, or herbs. Again, gently pat the chicken dry with paper towels or a kitchen towel reserved for handling raw meat.

Carefully remove the hot skillet from the oven and place it on top of the stove. Place the chicken, breast side up, in the skillet. You should hear it sizzle. Transfer the skillet back into the oven and roast for 20 minutes.

After 20 minutes, check the chicken; the skin should have started to bubble and blister. If the chicken appears to be burning or smoking, reduce the oven temperature by 25 degrees before returning the chicken to the oven.

After 10 minutes, remove the skillet from the oven and place it on a burner. Carefully turn the chicken over onto its breast, taking care not to tear the skin. This is best achieved with two wide, flat wooden spoons or spatulas.

continued on p. 68

EDITOR'S WINE CHOICE
Fruit-dense, focused white Burgundy.

SKILLET-ROASTED WHOLE CHICKEN *continued*

Return the chicken to the oven and roast for another 10 to 20 minutes, depending on the size of the bird. Finally, turn it back breast side up and roast for another 5 to 10 minutes to crisp the skin.

Check the chicken for doneness by inserting a meat thermometer into the meatiest part of the breast. It should register at least 165°F. If the chicken is not quite done, it will have to roast a while longer. But if the skin is already browned, cover the chicken with foil before returning it to the oven.

When the chicken is done, transfer it from the skillet to a plate and tent with foil. Pour off the clear fat from the skillet and reserve it for another use. To make a sauce from the pan drippings, add a few spoonfuls of water, stock, or white wine and put the skillet on a burner over low heat, using the back of a spoon to scrape up any crusty brown bits from the bottom of the pan.

Let the chicken rest for 10 to 15 minutes. Carve the chicken and serve with the pan drippings sauce.

The cooked chicken will keep in the refrigerator, tightly wrapped, for up to 3 days.

TIP FROM THE KITCHN
Make sure you measure out the ingredients and prep the spice rub before handling the raw chicken so you don't have to worry about cross-contamination.

LEMONY RICOTTA PASTA WITH BASIL

Total **30 min**; Serves **6**

Kosher salt

1 **pound gemelli**

2 **cups fresh ricotta cheese (1 pound)**

1 **cup freshly grated Parmigiano-Reggiano cheese**

2 **tablespoons extra-virgin olive oil**

Finely grated zest and juice of 1 lemon

Freshly ground pepper

½ **cup loosely packed basil leaves, cut into chiffonade**

EDITOR'S WINE CHOICE
Minerally, lemony Italian white, such as Verdicchio.

Because this recipe is so simple, Sara Kate Gillingham and Faith Durand urge you to use the best-quality ingredients: "If you can avoid the skim milk and commercially made ricottas, do," they advise. Short pastas such as rotini, penne, fusilli and gemelli are best for holding the sauce. "Again, quality makes a big difference here. Now's a time to spring for something better than plain-wrap spaghetti."

1. Bring a large pot of water to a boil and season generously with salt. Add the gemelli and cook until al dente.

2. Meanwhile, in a large heatproof bowl wide enough to fit over the pasta pot, stir the ricotta with the Parmigiano-Reggiano, olive oil and lemon zest and juice. Season with salt and pepper.

3. When the pasta is almost al dente, set the bowl of ricotta over the boiling water and stir until the ricotta is creamy. Remove the bowl. Drain the pasta and stir it into the ricotta until evenly coated. Transfer to a platter and sprinkle with the basil. Serve immediately.

FOR MORE ON SARA KATE GILLINGHAM & FAITH DURAND
thekitchn.com, faithdurand.com
☐ Sara Kate Gillingham
☐ @sarakategr, @faithdurand

CARLA'S COMFORT FOODS

Favorite Dishes from Around the World

BY CARLA HALL WITH GENEVIEVE KO

'm all about lovin' people," says Hall, the exuberant co-host of ABC's *The Chew.* Her book reflects that spirit: "I'm gonna take you from Nashville to Naples to Nigeria so you can taste and see how we're all united by great meals shared with family and friends." She weaves personal anecdotes into each of her recipes, describing, for instance, how the Vietnamese sandwiches she devoured between taping *Top Chef* episodes inspired her banh mi pork burgers (p. 72), or telling how a post-college trip to Seoul introduced her to the salty, sweet, garlicky flavors that make her soy-marinated short ribs so good (p. 74). She's a warm, chatty, ebullient presence. "It's like I'm cooking with you," she writes. "I wanted to say, 'Girlfriends, guy friends, let's go on a culinary adventure!'"

Published by Atria Books, $30

BANH MI PORK BURGERS WITH CARROTS & CILANTRO

Vietnamese
Serves **4**

- ½ cup julienned peeled carrots
- ½ cup julienned peeled daikon radish
- 2 teaspoons fresh lime juice
- 1 teaspoon sugar
- Kosher salt
- 1 pound ground pork
- ¼ cup very thinly sliced scallions (green onions)
- 1 tablespoon freshly grated lime zest
- 1 garlic clove, minced
- 1 teaspoon grated peeled fresh ginger
- Canola oil, for the pan
- Mayonnaise
- 4 brioche buns, split and toasted
- 12 fresh cilantro sprigs

Being a Top Chef *contestant can be grueling and exhausting and crazy fun. When we're all wiped out from nonstop competition, we do what we do best: eat good food. Some of my most memorable meals with those talented chefs involved banh mi, traditional Vietnamese sandwiches that layer cured meats, sausages, and pickled vegetables in small, soft versions of French baguettes. I love anything with pickles and fresh cilantro! I've put those flavors in a burger patty here and sandwiched them in my favorite French roll: buttery brioche. The rich bread makes all the difference, as does high-quality pork.*

1. In a medium bowl, toss the carrots, daikon, lime juice, sugar, and ½ teaspoon salt. Let stand while you make the burgers.

2. In a large bowl, combine the pork, scallions, lime zest, garlic, ginger, and ½ teaspoon salt with your hands until well mixed. Form into four ½-inch-thick patties that are slightly larger than your buns.

3. Heat a large cast-iron skillet over medium heat. Rub it with oil to coat. Add a few patties. They should fit comfortably in a single layer; don't crowd the pan. Cook until browned on the bottom, about 5 minutes, then flip and cook until the meat is cooked through, about 5 minutes longer. Repeat with the remaining patties.

4. Spread mayonnaise on both sides of the buns. Place a patty on each bottom bun, and top with the cilantro, carrots, and daikon. Sandwich with the top buns and serve immediately.

CARLA'S TIPS

To grate ginger without getting its stringy fibers, grate it lengthwise, along the fibers.

Swap Out: You can use ground dark meat chicken instead of pork.

Some Like It Hot: Squirt sriracha all over the burgers. And if you really like cilantro, mince a bunch and mix it with the mayo.

EDITOR'S BEER CHOICE
Citrusy, spiced wheat beer.

GRILLED SOY-MARINATED SHORT RIBS

Korean
Serves **10**

¾ **cup soy sauce**

¾ **cup water**

¾ **cup minced yellow onion**

¼ **cup minced garlic**

¼ **cup packed light or dark brown sugar**

3 **tablespoons cider vinegar**

2 **teaspoons toasted sesame oil**

1 **teaspoon freshly ground black pepper**

Twenty ½-inch-thick flanken-style short ribs (4⅓ pounds total)

The summer after my college graduation, I traveled to Seoul with my friend Lorrie and tasted Korean barbecue for the first time. I thought it was so cool to get to barbecue my meat myself, right on the tabletop. It was very festive, even though it was just the two of us at the table with tons of dishes. In lieu of a tabletop setup at home, I grill my ribs on my charcoal grill for a great smoky flavor, and on an indoor grill pan when I'm craving this in bad weather.

The salty, sweet marinade has a garlicky kick that comes through the char of the meat. The hardest part about this dish is buying the right ribs. Unlike short ribs cut for braising, these are cut into ½-inch-thick slices through three or four bones and are labeled "flanken-style" in Western markets and "L.A.-style" in Korean ones. At my local market, I asked my butcher to cut his whole slab of short ribs into the slices for me and he kindly did. I bet your butcher will do the same.

1. In a medium bowl, stir together the soy sauce, water, onion, garlic, brown sugar, vinegar, sesame oil, and pepper. Divide the ribs between two gallon-size heavy-duty resealable plastic bags, and then divide the marinade between the bags. Make sure the marinade is evenly distributed among the ribs. Seal tightly and refrigerate for at least 6 hours and up to overnight.

2. Prepare an outdoor grill for high-heat grilling (charcoal will make the tastiest ribs!), or heat a cast-iron skillet over medium-high heat. For both, cook the ribs, turning once, until nicely browned on both sides, about 5 minutes total. Serve with short-grain white rice and kimchi.

SHORT RIBS

This magic cut of meat packs so much flavor. I love that you can cook down big pieces until they're fork-tender or quick-grill thin slices for ribs with a pleasant chew. The richness takes to just about any seasoning, but simple is better here. Short ribs have been all the rage in restaurants in recent years, but I think they're worth doing at home. The hardest part is buying the right cut. For the braises here, you want 3-inch squares with the bone in. That means that if a butcher has a whole rack of short ribs, he needs to cut between the bones, then cut across the bones to form 3-inch square pieces. For the grilled dish, the butcher will have to cut across the whole rack, through all 3 or 4 of the bones, making ½-inch-wide slices.

EDITOR'S WINE CHOICE
Juicy, blackberry-rich Argentinean Malbec.

ROASTED GREEN BEANS WITH BASIL

Italian
Serves **4**

1 pound green beans, trimmed

8 garlic cloves, unpeeled, ends trimmed

3 tablespoons extra-virgin olive oil

1 small yellow onion, cut in half and then into ¼-inch-thick half-moons

Kosher salt

¼ cup sliced fresh basil leaves

1 teaspoon fresh lemon juice

My motto for roasting green beans: the hotter, the quicker, the better. They get nice and charred and there's great flavor in that brown. If there's anything I've learned about Italian food from my Chew *co-host Mario Batali, it's that vegetables should be treated simply to let their natural sweetness shine. This recipe does just that.*

1. Preheat the oven to 450°F. Toss the green beans and garlic cloves with 2 tablespoons of the oil on a rimmed baking sheet. Arrange them in a single layer on one side of the pan. Arrange the onion slices in a single layer on the other side of the pan and rub with the remaining 1 tablespoon oil. Sprinkle ½ teaspoon salt over everything. Roast until the green beans are browned and tender, about 25 minutes.

2. Squeeze the garlic cloves out of their skins into a large bowl, and mash them. Then add the green beans, onions, basil, and ¼ teaspoon salt. Toss well, then toss in the lemon juice and serve.

GREEN BEANS

Yes, green beans can be great raw...and even what some might call overcooked. I never say never when trying dishes and have figured out a way to make classic super-soft American green beans great. On the other end of the spectrum, I've kept them crunchy as pickles. And right in the middle, I've blazed them in a hot oven.

For all of my rustic treatments, be sure to start with good ol' American beans and not the slender, forest-green French haricots verts. I wash my beans well first, in case there's any grit, then I tip and tail them. While I find it therapeutic to snap both ends one by one, ideally on a sunny porch, I often don't have time for that. The fastest way to trim green beans is to bunch up a handful and line up their stem ends, then slice straight across. I like to do the tails too: line up the other ends and cut off those little suckers.

SPICED ROASTED CAULIFLOWER

Indian
Serves **4**

- 1 teaspoon garam masala
- ½ teaspoon cumin seeds
- ¼ teaspoon ground coriander
- ¼ teaspoon cayenne pepper
- 2 tablespoons unsalted butter
- 2 tablespoons canola oil
- Kosher salt
- 1 large (2½-pound) cauliflower, cored and cut into small florets
- Lime wedges

When I think Indian food, I think spice. So the first time I did this dish, I went a little overboard and I learned that Indian food is about spice, but not about hitting you over the head with it. Now I've got the balance just right for cauliflower that's been thrown into a super-hot oven where its natural sweetness intensifies as the florets caramelize. After my initial misfire on this dish, I also found that a combo of butter and oil works best: The butter adds richness and the oil helps the browning. This blend delivers the fragrant flavors of the spices, making it ideal for any roasted vegetables.

1. Preheat the oven to 425°F. Combine the garam masala, cumin, coriander, and cayenne in a small skillet. Toast over medium-high heat, shaking the skillet occasionally, until fragrant, 1 to 2 minutes. Remove from the heat and add the butter, oil, and 1 teaspoon salt. Stir until the butter melts.

2. Toss the cauliflower with the spiced butter on a rimmed baking sheet until well coated. Spread the cauliflower out in a single layer and roast until tender and browned, about 15 minutes. Season to taste with salt and lime juice.

CAULIFLOWER
Its mildness is what makes cauliflower great for my style of cooking with big, deep flavors. This pale cruciferous vegetable takes to just about any seasoning, so I load it up with my favorite combos. Look for heads that are unblemished, with leaves tightly tucked under the compact florets. Snap off the leaves, then trim the thick bottom stem before prepping. The real key to good cauliflower is to start by cooking it properly. Undercooked and it'll be hard; overcooked and it gets that smelly funk. A cake tester or a sharp, thin knife works best for checking doneness. It should slide through the stem with just a hint of resistance.

FETA MAC & CHEESE WITH CRUNCHY TOMATO-OLIVE CRUMBS

Active **40 min**; Total **1 hr 30 min**; Serves **6**

2 tablespoons pine nuts

1 pint grape tomatoes

3 tablespoons extra-virgin olive oil

Kosher salt and pepper

¼ baguette (4 ounces), torn into ½-inch chunks

¼ cup slivered pitted kalamata olives

1 teaspoon fresh oregano leaves, finely chopped

3 tablespoons unsalted butter

3 tablespoons all-purpose flour

3 cups whole milk

¼ cup minced yellow onion

2 garlic cloves, minced

2 bay leaves

1 teaspoon dried oregano

Finely grated zest of 1 lemon

1 large egg, lightly beaten

10 ounces feta cheese, crumbled (2½ cups)

½ pound elbow macaroni

EDITOR'S WINE CHOICE
Zippy, fruit-forward California Sauvignon Blanc.

"During a segment of The Chew, *my co-host Michael Symon made the most delicious Greek baked feta," Carla Hall recalls. "I thought those flavors would be amazing in a mac and cheese."*

1. Preheat the oven to 400°F. Spread the pine nuts on a foil-lined baking sheet and bake for 4 minutes, until golden brown. Transfer to a medium bowl and let cool. On the same baking sheet, toss the tomatoes with 1 tablespoon of the olive oil and ¼ teaspoon each of salt and pepper; push them to one side of the baking sheet. On the other side, toss the baguette chunks with the remaining 2 tablespoons of olive oil and ½ teaspoon salt. Bake until the tomatoes collapse and the bread is golden brown, about 10 minutes. Transfer the baking sheet to a rack and let cool. Add the tomatoes to the pine nuts along with the olives and fresh oregano. Reduce the oven temperature to 375°F.

2. Meanwhile, bring a large pot of water to a boil and season generously with salt. In a large saucepan, melt the butter over moderate heat. Whisk in the flour and cook for 2 minutes. Whisk in the milk until incorporated, then stir in the onion, garlic, bay leaves, dried oregano and lemon zest. Bring to a boil, then reduce the heat to moderately low and cook, stirring, until thickened, about 8 minutes. Remove from the heat and discard the bay leaves. Whisk in the egg until smooth. Stir in 2 cups of the feta and season generously with salt and pepper.

3. Add the macaroni to the boiling water and cook for 2 minutes. Drain the macaroni and stir it into the cheese sauce until evenly coated. Scrape into an 8-inch square baking dish and smooth the top. Bake for 30 minutes, until bubbly. Remove from the oven. Sprinkle with the remaining ½ cup of feta and the tomato–pine nut–olive mixture, then cover with the croutons. Bake the mac and cheese for 5 minutes, until the toppings are piping hot.

FOR MORE ON CARLA HALL
carlahall.com
Chef Carla Hall
@carlahall

Gabrielle Hamilton (far right) opened her groundbreaking restaurant Prune in Manhattan's East Village in 1999.

PRUNE

BY GABRIELLE HAMILTON

In this long-awaited recipe collection, the New York City chef and memoirist Gabrielle Hamilton sets out to create an entirely new kind of cookbook. Hers reads like a manual for young chefs starting out in Prune's kitchen, where space is a luxury no one can afford and stove burners vary wildly in heat. The book comes complete with sauce-splattered pages, masking-tape markings in the margins to show doubled and quadrupled amounts for multiple batches and special notes written only in important circumstances. She warns the cooks, for example, to take particular care in plating the salt-packed roast beef with bread crumb salsa (p. 84): "Let the perfect wall-to-wall pink of the filet show—don't hide that beauty under carelessly placed salsa." Hamilton's recipes reflect her persona: eccentric and sometimes acidic, but always balanced in the familiar and aiming for maximum pleasure.

Published by Random House, $45

AVOCADO SANDWICH WITH LEMON RICOTTA

Yield **4 orders**

1 **pound/scant 2 cups fresh ricotta**

Zest of 2 lemons

¼ **cup extra-virgin olive oil, plus more for drizzling**

Kosher salt

Freshly ground black pepper

4 **long, even slices peasant bread**

2 **large, perfectly ripe avocados—at room temperature**

1 **dry pint mixed-colors grape tomatoes, rinsed and cut in half horizontally**

8 **red pearl onions, thinly sliced into rounds**

4 **teaspoons toasted sesame seeds**

Skin of 1 preserved lemon, flesh and pith removed, finely diced

½ **teaspoon toasted poppy seeds**

Maldon sea salt

EDITOR'S WINE CHOICE
Vibrant, lemon-inflected Italian white, such as Vermentino.

Mix ricotta with lemon zest, ¼ cup EVOO, salt, and pepper and set aside.

Arrange slices of bread on the cutting board and divide the ricotta mixture evenly among the 4 slices. Spread into a generous even layer.

Split the avocados, remove the pits, and slice each half into even slices without cutting all the way through the leathery skin. Then, with a soup spoon or a flexible rubber spatula, release the flesh and arrange the slices neatly and evenly among the bread.

Artfully and attractively arrange the tomatoes by nesting them into the soft avocado. Then neatly arrange the red onion slices over the tomatoes.

Garnish each sandwich with sesame seeds, preserved lemon zest, and, finally, the poppy seeds.

Transfer the sandwiches to plates and then drizzle with the extra-virgin olive oil. Sprinkle few grains of Maldon sea salt.

SALT-PACKED COLD ROAST BEEF WITH BREAD CRUMB SALSA

Yield **6 orders**

FOR THE BEEF

- 24 **ounces trimmed and clean beef tenderloin**
- 1 **Tablespoon grapeseed oil**
- 2 **teaspoons finely and freshly ground black pepper**
- 2 **pounds kosher salt (Diamond Crystal only)**
- 1½ **cups cold water**

FOR THE BREAD CRUMB SALSA

- 1 **cup EVOO**
- 6 **ounces day-old peasant bread, torn into free-form small-ish "croutons"**
- 1 **pound assorted sweet cherry tomatoes, split in half**
- 1 **bunch scallions, sliced thinly in rings, from the white all the way up through as much of the green stalk as is edible**
- 4 **small cloves fresh and sticky new garlic, thinly sliced**
- 1 **packed Tablespoon plus 1 packed teaspoon salt-packed anchovies, rinsed, filleted, and then minced**
- 2 **lemons, zested, supremed, deseeded, and all the juice from what's left of the skeleton after supreming the segments**
- 2 **Tablespoons red wine vinegar**
- ½ **cup clean and dry flat-leaf Italian parsley leaves**

FOR THE BEEF:

Heat the large, heavy cast-iron skillet over medium heat for 5 whole minutes and make sure the hood is on.

Rub the filet with 1 Tablespoon of oil, then sprinkle and coat evenly with black pepper.

Brown the meat thoroughly on every side and also the cut ends so that you have formed a nice crust universally around the piece of filet, creating a barrier for the upcoming salt crust. (This takes 7 to 8 minutes to brown correctly.)

Remove the meat from the pan and let cool on a wire rack set in a sheet pan—in order to have a cool and mostly dry piece of meat.

Mix the salt with the water to form what looks like bright white wet sand.

Spread a thin but solid and even layer of salt on the bottom of a ¼ sheet pan and set the roast on it, then pack the remaining moist salt tidily around the browned meat forming a solid case, resembling a cast on a broken leg. Where there are cracks, redistribute the salt and fix them. This should be a fun and unfussy task. If you need more salt or more water or less water and more salt, mix up whatever mortar you need to get the beef encased.

Place the salt-crusted beef on its sheet pan into 250° oven and let it cook for 45 minutes. If you weighed it properly at the outset, 45 minutes at 250° is failsafe. Otherwise, use an instaread thermometer and go in through a cut end to direct center—pull it when it hits 125° inside.

Crack the salt crust, dust the granules of clinging salt off with a clean dry side towel, and set to rest on a tray in your station. Don't refrigerate, but label properly time/date for Health Department.

FOR THE BREAD CRUMB SALSA:

In a small, deep-sided sauté pan, heat the 1 cup of olive oil over medium-high heat. The oil should be just deep enough to submerge the first tip of your index finger. Good olive oil is rarely recommended for frying so don't ever do this when you go on to work in a real restaurant, but here at Prune, I really prefer the flavor it adds.

When the oil makes its beautiful, veinous, streaking patterns in the pan, which will move faster as the oil gets hotter, drop in a test piece of crouton. When it sizzles on contact, the oil is ready.

Fry the croutons until golden brown, remove with a slotted spoon, and drain in stack of basket-style coffee filters. Set aside the frying oil to cool.

Mix together the tomatoes, scallions, garlic, anchovies, lemon flesh and zest and juice, and the red wine vinegar and toss well.

Toss in the fried bread croutons and dress with ⅓ cup of the now-cool olive oil left over from frying.

Rough up the parsley leaves briefly in your hands just to release the grassy aroma and add to the salsa.

Sparingly season with salt and pepper to taste, keeping in mind that the filet will bring its own seasoning to the plate.

TO PLATE:
Slice the beef to order, keep portion at 6 ounces.

Shingle meat.

Drape good big spoonful of salsa over meat—but let the perfect wall-to-wall pink of the filet show—don't hide that beauty under carelessly placed salsa.

Drizzle with some of the remaining fry oil to finish.

Do not season further.

EDITOR'S WINE CHOICE
Bold, Tempranillo-based red from Rioja.

GRILLED LAMB BLADE CHOPS

Yield **6 orders**

2 cups kosher salt

1 gallon water

6 branches rosemary

¼ cup black peppercorns

6 lamb blade chops,
   1½ inches thick

Extra-virgin olive oil
(Kalamata olive varietal)

Dried Greek oregano

Dissolve salt in ½ gallon warm water. Add ½ gallon very cold water. Add fresh rosemary, roughed up briefly in your hands to release the oils a bit. Just crush or bruise the black peppercorns under a cast-iron skillet, then add to brine. Submerge the lamb chops in brine and refrigerate 24 hours. Remove lamb from brine. Rinse and dry. Let chops rest at room temperature, 20 minutes.

Run with skordalia and Piyaz in cold months.
" with braised dandies in spring.
" with Greek Salad ONLY IN SUMMER.

TO PICK UP:
Rub chops with olive oil sparingly. Season with salt and pepper and dried Greek oregano. Grill blade chops until solidly medium rare. (Because of all of the muscles that come together across the shoulder, these chops are too tough and chewy any rarer.) Plate the chop when cooked, let it rest on serving plate for juices to collect. Don't hold these on a sizzle in your station—I like the rested juices to make their way to the customer, like they would at home.

when you rest your meats on a sizzle plate in The midst of all that greasy soot coming off The grill, the juices mostly evaporate and get crusty on The sizzle plate and I am really repulsed by That. Please get The meat from The heat to The plate without any intermediary shuffling around in your station.
   Even though you are a line cook in a busy restaurant, try to cook like you would at home. Nobody rests their meat at home over a hot, burning, dirty grill and we shouldn't either.
   PLEASE DO NOT:
      pre-mark
      misfire
      poorly time
      weight down/press down
      flash under the sally
ANY OF THE MEAT HERE.

EDITOR'S WINE CHOICE
Herby, berry-dense southern Rhône red.

FOR MORE ON GABRIELLE HAMILTON
prunerestaurant.com
[f] Prune

VIBRANT FOOD

Celebrating the Ingredients, Recipes & Colors of Each Season

BY KIMBERLEY HASSELBRINK

Kimberley Hasselbrink began thinking about color as a way to "reinvigorate her relationship with food" while in art school: "It was a head of overripe purple cauliflower—the last from my friend Nicole's winter garden—that began my obsession with colorful produce." On her blog, The Year in Food, and now in her thoughtful first cookbook, she uses the pigments of each season's produce to build gorgeous, simple, wheat-free dishes with unexpected combinations of flavor and texture, as in a silky red pepper soup with feta and cumin-toasted pumpkin seeds (p. 92). Photos accompany every recipe, inspiring readers to heed Hasselbrink's call to action: "Perhaps you'll bring a striking vegetable home and mull over it, and then build a colorful dish around that vegetable. That is how I cook."

Published by Ten Speed Press, $25

APRICOT & CHICKEN SALAD WITH TOASTED CUMIN VINAIGRETTE

Serves **4 to 6**

TOASTED CUMIN VINAIGRETTE

- **1 tablespoon cumin seeds**
- **2 tablespoons freshly squeezed lemon juice**
- **2 tablespoons brown rice vinegar**
- **1 teaspoon honey**
- **¾ teaspoon sweet paprika**
- **¼ teaspoon fine sea salt, plus more to taste**
- **¼ cup extra-virgin olive oil**
- **1½ tablespoons finely chopped fresh cilantro leaves**
- **1 tablespoon finely chopped fresh flat-leaf parsley**
- **Freshly ground black pepper**

- **½ cup sliced raw almonds**
- **2 cups shredded cooked chicken (about 10 ounces)**
- **4 fresh apricots (about 8 ounces), pitted and sliced**
- **6 cups loosely packed wild arugula**

EDITOR'S WINE CHOICE
Vibrant, full-bodied South African Chenin Blanc.

Apricots can be so fussy. At their peak, they are heavenly, marvelous fruit, but so often what's available at the supermarket is underripe and a little bland. Go for fragrant, rosy gold apricots at the peak of their season. The vibrant flavors of cumin and green herbs make this salad really sing. It's great as a hearty weekday lunch.

To make the vinaigrette, in a small frying pan over medium-low heat, toast the cumin seeds until golden and fragrant, about 3 minutes, stirring regularly. Grind the seeds in a spice grinder or mortar and pestle. In a bowl, whisk together the lemon juice, vinegar, honey, cumin, paprika, and salt. Gradually whisk in the oil until the vinaigrette is emulsified. Whisk in the cilantro and parsley. Season with pepper.

To make the salad, in the same small frying pan, toast the almonds over medium-low heat, stirring often, until golden and fragrant, about 4 minutes. Set aside to cool.

In a large serving bowl, toss together the chicken, apricots, half of the almonds, and the arugula. Drizzle with 3 to 4 tablespoons of the vinaigrette and toss gently until the vinaigrette is evenly distributed. Garnish with the remaining almonds and season to taste with more salt if desired. Serve with the remaining vinaigrette on the side. Store any leftover vinaigrette in an airtight container in the refrigerator for up to 3 days.

SMOKY RED PEPPER SOUP WITH PUMPKIN SEEDS & FETA

Serves **4**

3 pounds red bell peppers
(4 to 6 peppers)

1 tablespoon plus 1 teaspoon
extra-virgin olive oil

1 small red onion, diced

2 cloves garlic, minced

1 teaspoon sweet paprika

1 teaspoon smoked paprika

1 teaspoon fine sea salt

¼ teaspoon ground chipotle
chile powder

4 cups low-sodium
vegetable broth

¼ cup raw, shelled
pumpkin seeds

¼ teaspoon ground cumin

½ cup crumbled feta cheese

I love what fire does to a pepper, making it lusciously smoky and rich. This soup takes the essence of a pepper and concentrates it. Peppers are one of those ingredients whose color is hardly diminished by cooking. I find that I need texture in a blended soup; this one is rounded out with pumpkin seeds toasted in cumin and a few chunks of salty feta cheese.

Preheat the broiler.

Arrange the peppers in a single layer on a baking sheet. Broil 6 to 8 inches from the heat for 15 to 20 minutes, turning every few minutes, until the peppers are mostly blackened. Remove from the broiler and set aside to cool.

When the peppers are cool enough to handle, remove the skins under running water. Pull the stems from the peppers and rinse out the seeds. Coarsely chop the peppers and set aside.

Warm 1 tablespoon of the oil in a large stockpot. Add the onions and sauté for 3 minutes, stirring occasionally. Add the garlic and sauté for another minute. Stir in the sweet and smoked paprika, salt, and chipotle powder. Add the broth and the red peppers and bring to a boil. Reduce the heat to low, cover, and simmer for 15 minutes.

In a small pan over medium heat, add the remaining 1 teaspoon of olive oil. Add the pumpkin seeds and the cumin and sauté until toasted, 3 to 4 minutes, stirring regularly. Set aside.

Purée the soup using an immersion blender or food processor. To serve, top each bowl with the toasted pumpkin seeds and crumbled feta cheese.

CHILE-ROASTED DELICATA SQUASH WITH QUESO FRESCO

Serves **4**

2 delicata squash
(about 1½ pounds)

3 tablespoons plus 1 teaspoon
extra-virgin olive oil

1 tablespoon maple syrup

½ teaspoon ground cumin

¼ to ½ teaspoon chipotle
chile powder

¼ teaspoon sweet paprika

¼ teaspoon fine sea salt,
plus more to taste

¼ cup crumbled queso fresco

2 tablespoons coarsely
chopped fresh cilantro

Delicata is my favorite of the winter squash. It's sweeter and, as its name implies, more delicate than other squash. Plus, you don't have to peel it. I enjoy the graceful scalloped edges that are made when you slice through the squash crosswise. The simple combination of smoky chipotle powder, fresh cilantro, and queso fresco perfectly balances the caramelized squash.

Preheat the oven to 400°F.

Slice the squash in half crosswise. Scoop out the seeds and pulp, discarding the pulp. Rinse the seeds and set aside to drain. Slice each squash half into ¼-inch to ½-inch rounds.

In a large mixing bowl, combine the 3 tablespoons olive oil, maple syrup, cumin, chipotle powder, paprika, and salt. Add the squash and toss to thoroughly coat. Arrange the squash in a single layer on a large baking sheet, overlapping the slices slightly if necessary.

On a separate baking sheet, toss the squash seeds with the remaining 1 teaspoon of olive oil and a light sprinkle of salt.

Place the squash and seeds in the oven. Roast the squash for 20 to 25 minutes, turning the slices halfway. Check on the seeds after 10 minutes and remove from the oven when golden brown. The squash will be ready when fork-tender, golden brown, and caramelized.

Place the squash on a large serving dish. Sprinkle the toasted seeds, queso fresco, and cilantro leaves over the squash. This dish is best served warm.

FOR MORE ON KIMBERLEY HASSELBRINK
kimberleyhasselbrink.com, theyearinfood.com
The Year in Food
@theyearinfood

ISRAELI CHICKEN
WITH MOGHRABIEH,
HARISSA-GRILLED
PEACHES & MINT, P. 102

A CHANGE OF APPETITE

Where Healthy Meets Delicious

BY DIANA HENRY

Being a food writer can be very bad for your health, unless you have the resolve of a saint," concedes Diana Henry, who writes a weekly column for the *Sunday Telegraph*'s magazine in London. After a lifetime of fad diets ("I have spent so much energy angsting about them I could weep") and 15 years as a professional eater, she became drawn toward what she calls "accidentally healthy" foods—dishes that are, first and foremost, delicious. She references the Middle East and North Africa in many of her recipes, like a brilliantly spiced lentil and roasted tomato soup with harissa (p. 100), but she also looks for ideas everywhere from Japan to Bulgaria. "This is good food for people who love eating," Henry says. "It's a great bonus that it's good for you as well."

Published by Mitchell Beazley, $35

BULGARIAN GRILLED ZUCCHINI & EGGPLANTS WITH TARATOR

FOR THE TARATOR

- 1 slice of country-style bread
- 2 garlic cloves
- 1 cup walnuts, plus extra to serve
- ½ cup extra-virgin olive oil, plus extra to serve
- Juice of ½ lemon
- Salt and black pepper
- ⅔ cup Greek yogurt
- 2 tablespoons chopped dill leaves, plus extra to serve

FOR THE GRILLED VEGETABLES

- 5 large mixed green and yellow zucchini
- 2 large eggplants
- Olive oil

EDITOR'S WINE CHOICE
Ripe, slightly nutty Italian white, such as Soave.

Tarator—a nut-based sauce—appears in different guises in Bulgaria, Turkey, and Greece. It can be made with hazelnuts, walnuts, almonds, or pine nuts and is just as good with a salad of raw cucumber, greens, herbs, and tomatoes as it is with cooked vegetables. It also keeps well in the refrigerator for a day or so; just take it out and let it come to room temperature before serving, otherwise it gets a bit solid.

Tear the bread into pieces and put it into a food processor with the garlic and walnuts. Puree while adding the extra-virgin oil and lemon juice. Add the seasoning and the yogurt with ¼ cup of water and puree again. Stir in the dill, taste, and adjust the seasoning. Put into a bowl and set aside until you're ready to serve (or cover and put in the refrigerator).

Trim each end from the zucchini and slice lengthwise about ⅛ inch thick. Remove the stems from the eggplants and cut them widthwise into slices of the same thickness as the zucchini. Brush all the sliced vegetables on both sides with regular olive oil.

Heat a ridged grill pan and cook the slices of zucchini on both sides until golden brown and soft. You will need to do this in batches. Do the same with the eggplants, making sure they get a good color on each side, then reduce the heat until the slices are soft and cooked through. Season the vegetables as you cook them.

Put the vegetables onto a serving plate, drizzling with a little extra-virgin oil. Spoon some of the tarator over them (offer the rest in a bowl) and sprinkle with more walnuts and dill.

GOOD SON-IN-LAW EGGS

Serves **8**

8 **eggs**

2 **tablespoons peanut oil**

6 **shallots, finely sliced**

2 **tablespoons tamarind paste**

2 **tablespoons Thai fish sauce**

2 **tablespoons packed light brown sugar**

3 **tablespoons chopped cilantro leaves**

2 **red chiles, seeded and finely chopped**

In authentic son-in-law eggs, hard-boiled eggs are fried before being sauced. It contributes to the texture, but I'll forgo that to eat something that hasn't been fried and yet offers wonderful contrasts. These are eggs you would give a good son-in-law (because you want him to be healthy).

Hard boil the eggs for seven minutes, drain, and let sit in the warm saucepan with a lid on.

Meanwhile, heat the oil and cook the shallots over medium heat until golden brown and slightly crispy. Set half aside. To the other half, add the tamarind, fish sauce, sugar, and ½ cup of water. Bring to a boil and cook for about three minutes; the sauce will reduce and become slightly syrupy.

Shell the eggs and put them in bowls. Spoon some sauce over them and sprinkle with the remaining shallots, the cilantro, and chiles.

NOTE
You are supposed to serve these with jasmine rice (and they are fabulous) but they're also good with brown rice. I love to top the rice with stir-fried greens or baby spinach or watercress (the leaves wilt in the heat of the sauce) to make a more complete meal.

LENTIL & ROASTED TOMATO SOUP WITH SAFFRON

Serves **6**

10 plum tomatoes, halved

¼ cup olive oil

2 teaspoons harissa

Salt and black pepper

2 teaspoons brown sugar (optional)

2 teaspoons cumin seeds

1 teaspoon coriander seeds

1 tablespoon peanut oil

1 large onion, chopped

4 garlic cloves, chopped

½ teaspoon turmeric

Good pinch of saffron stamens

¾ inch piece ginger root, chopped

1 green chile, finely chopped

1 cup split red lentils

3¾ cups vegetable stock

¼ cup chopped cilantro leaves

Plain yogurt (optional)

Toasted slivered almonds

The tomatoes give real depth. It makes a hearty opener, but the main course is deceptively light.

Preheat the oven to 375°F. Put the tomatoes in a roasting pan in which they can lie in a single layer. Mix together the olive oil, harissa, and salt and black pepper in a small bowl and pour the mixture over the tomatoes. Turn over to coat, ending with the tomatoes cut side up. (If your tomatoes aren't the best, sprinkle the brown sugar over them, but their natural sweetness comes out as they roast.) Cook for 45 minutes, until slightly shrunken and charred in places. Set aside the six nicest looking tomato halves.

Toast the cumin and coriander seeds for two minutes in a dry pan. Grind them in a mortar and set aside. Heat the peanut oil in a saucepan and sauté the onion until soft and golden brown. Add the garlic, all the spices, ginger, and chile and cook for two minutes. Add the lentils, stirring to coat in the cooking juices, tomatoes with their juices, and the stock. Season well. Bring to a boil, reduce the heat to a simmer, and cook for 15 to 20 minutes, or until the lentils have collapsed into a puree. The tomatoes should have disintegrated, too. Now either puree the soup or keep it chunky. Check the seasoning and stir in most of the cilantro. Serve each bowlful with a swirl of yogurt (if you want), a reserved tomato half, a few toasted almonds, and some of the remaining cilantro.

ISRAELI CHICKEN WITH MOGHRABIEH, HARISSA-GRILLED PEACHES & MINT

Serves **4**

FOR THE CHICKEN AND MOGHRABIEH

- **⅓ cup hot mustard (I use English mustard)**
- **8 skinless bone-in chicken thighs (or other chicken joints)**
- **3 tablespoons packed dark brown sugar**
- **Salt and black pepper**
- **3 tablespoons olive oil**
- **⅓ cup orange juice**
- **1 cup whole-wheat moghrabieh (Lebanese couscous)**
- **1 tablespoon extra-virgin olive oil**
- **Good squeeze of lemon juice**

FOR THE PEACHES

- **3 just-ripe peaches, halved and pitted**
- **2 tablespoons olive oil**
- **3 tablespoons harissa, or to taste (reduce the amount if you want it less hot)**
- **Juice of ½ lemon**
- **Leaves from 1 small bunch of mint, torn**

EDITOR'S WINE CHOICE
Peach-inflected, full-bodied Rhône-style white, such as Viognier.

The chicken here is based on a recipe in Paula Wolfert's excellent book Mediterranean Cooking. *(If you don't own anything by Paula Wolfert, seek her out. Her books are full of dishes that are "accidentally" healthy.)*

Moghrabieh (Middle Eastern giant couscous), or Lebanese couscous, is difficult to find, but Amazon sells it. You could also use Israeli couscous, sometimes called pearl couscous, or matfoul, a bulgur wheat product, and cook it in the same way. Either can be used as a salad base.

Preheat the oven to 375°F.

Spread the mustard on both sides of the chicken thighs and put them into a small roasting pan or gratin dish in which they will fit snugly. Sprinkle with half the sugar and season. Drizzle with 2 tablespoons of the regular olive oil and all the orange juice. Roast in the oven for 20 minutes. Take the pan out, turn the chicken over, baste it, and sprinkle with the rest of the sugar. Season and return to the oven for another 15 minutes. The chicken should be dark gold.

When the chicken has about 15 minutes of cooking time left, turn to the moghrabieh. Heat the final 1 tablespoon of regular oil in a saucepan, add the moghrabieh, and stir over medium heat until golden brown; after about four minutes, you should be able to smell it getting toasted. Cover with boiling water, season, and simmer gently for about 10 minutes, until the moghrabieh is tender. Drain, toss with the extra-virgin oil and the lemon, and season.

Meanwhile, cut the peach halves into wedges and toss in a bowl with the 2 tablespoons of regular olive oil and the harissa. Heat a ridged grill pan until it is really hot. Lift the peach slices out of the harissa mixture, shaking off the excess, and cook on both sides until tender. Remove from the pan and squeeze lemon juice on top. Once the moghrabieh is ready, toss it with the peaches and mint. Serve with the chicken.

STRAWBERRY, TOMATO & BASIL SALAD

Total **20 min**; Serves **6**

Diana Henry gives strawberries a savory boost with tomatoes and fresh basil. Then she amplifies the "sharp-sweet" flavor by combining two types of vinegar for the dressing: fruity raspberry vinegar and white balsamic, which is less sweet and syrupy than red.

- 3 tablespoons raspberry vinegar (preferably one with raspberry pulp in it)
- 1½ tablespoons white balsamic vinegar
- 1 tablespoon superfine sugar
- 1 pound strawberries, hulled and halved (quartered if large)
- 1 pint small cherry or grape tomatoes, halved (quartered if large)
- 1 cup lightly packed basil leaves, torn
- Salt and pepper

EDITOR'S WINE CHOICE
Robust, berry-rich southern Italian rosé.

In a wide, shallow bowl, whisk together the vinegars and sugar until the sugar dissolves. Add the strawberries and tomatoes and toss well, then toss in the basil. Season the salad with salt and pepper. Let stand for 3 minutes to let the flavors mingle before serving.

FOR MORE ON DIANA HENRY
dianahenry.co.uk
@DianaHenryFood

The mayor and city council of Oakland, California, declared June 5, 2012, Tanya Holland Day for the chef's "significant role in creating community and establishing Oakland as a culinary center."

BROWN SUGAR KITCHEN

New-Style, Down-Home Recipes from Sweet West Oakland

BY TANYA HOLLAND WITH JAN NEWBERRY

Soul food prepared with French technique and a Northern Californian insistence on fresh, local ingredients—for chef Tanya Holland of Brown Sugar Kitchen, that translates to recipes like gougères with flecks of smoky andouille sausage (p. 106) and crispy chicken wings baked with cayenne and honey (p. 108). Against all expectations (including her own), the Bobby Flay protégé launched her restaurant in West Oakland, an area many outsiders consider sketchy. But tying together the wonderful recipes in her book is the story of a scrappy neighborhood with astonishing cultural diversity. Holland's success has been in bringing together the residents of West Oakland. As she writes, "The restaurant is an anchor for the neighborhood, a canteen for the artists, truckers and tradesmen who work here." *Brown Sugar Kitchen* is as much a story of urban revival as it is a cookbook.

Published by Chronicle Books, $30

ANDOUILLE GOUGÈRES

Makes **about two dozen gougères**

1 cup/240 ml water

½ cup/115 g unsalted butter

  Kosher salt

1 cup/125 g all-purpose flour

5 eggs

2½ oz/70 g Gruyère cheese, grated

4 oz/115 g andouille sausage, chopped

Gougères are sophisticated cheese puffs and are the appetizer of choice in Burgundy, France, where I went to cooking school. They're made from a base known as pâte à choux, a very elementary dough and one of the first I learned to make. Don't be intimidated by the fancy French name. Pâte à choux is easy to master and versatile too. It's the foundation for many famous pastries including éclairs and cream puffs, and as you see here, it also comes in handy for savory treats. For this Cajun-inspired version, I decided that a crumble of spicy andouille might just put them over the top.

Preheat the oven to 425°F/220°C. Line two baking sheets with parchment paper.

In a large saucepan, combine the water, butter, and ½ tsp salt. Bring to a boil over medium-high heat. When the butter has melted, add the flour all at once, stirring vigorously with a wooden spoon. Reduce the heat to medium, and keep stirring until the mixture has formed a smooth, thick paste and pulls away from the sides of the pan, about 3 minutes. Transfer to the bowl of a stand mixer fitted with the paddle attachment or to a large heatproof bowl.

If using a stand mixer, add 4 eggs, one at a time, mixing on low speed until the egg is incorporated and the dough is smooth before adding the next egg. (If mixing by hand, add 4 eggs, one at a time, stirring with a wooden spoon until the egg is incorporated and the dough is smooth before adding the next egg.) The mixture should be very thick, smooth, and shiny. Stir in the Gruyère and andouille. (To make ahead, cover the bowl tightly with plastic wrap and refrigerate for up to 1 day.)

Use a tablespoon to drop the dough into 1-in/2.5-cm rounds about 1½ in/4 cm apart on the prepared baking sheets. You should have about 2 dozen gougères.

In a small bowl, whisk the remaining egg with a pinch of salt to make an egg wash. Brush the top of each gougère with the egg wash.

Bake for 15 minutes. Reduce the oven to 375°F/190°C, rotate the baking sheets, and continue baking until the gougères are puffed and nicely browned, about 15 minutes more.

Serve warm or at room temperature.

(Baked gougères can be frozen for up to 1 month. Reheat in a 350°F/180°C oven for 8 to 10 minutes.)

EDITOR'S WINE CHOICE
Crisp, juicy sparkling wine, such as Prosecco.

SPICY BAKED WINGS

Makes **about 20 wings**

Vegetable oil for the baking sheets

4 lb/1.8 kg whole chicken wings or 3 lb/1.4 kg trimmed

1 tbsp dry mustard

1 tsp ground ginger

1 tsp kosher salt

1 tsp freshly ground black pepper

¼ tsp ground allspice

¼ tsp cayenne pepper

4 tbsp/55 g unsalted butter

4 large garlic cloves, minced

1 tbsp sauce from canned chipotle chiles in adobo

2 tsp Tabasco sauce

2 tbsp Crystal hot sauce

⅔ cup/225 g honey

The search for great chicken wings is over. We serve these at our sister restaurant, B-Side BBQ, and it's one of those dishes that always get a big reaction (like Phil jumping up and down). Great wings make people happy. These are perfect for game night or for no particular reason at all. The beauty is that they're baked and gluten-free and you can adjust the seasoning to your taste. Wings have become so popular that markets now sell them trimmed and ready to use, often labeled "party wings."

Preheat the oven to 425°F/220°C. Line two large rimmed baking sheets with aluminum foil and lightly coat with oil.

If using whole wings, separate the sections of chicken wings at the joints, discarding or saving the wing tip portion for another use.

In a large bowl, combine the mustard, ginger, salt, black pepper, allspice, and cayenne.

In a small saucepan, melt the butter over medium heat. Add the garlic and cook until the garlic is fragrant and softened, about 2 minutes. Stir in the chipotle sauce, Tabasco sauce, Crystal hot sauce, and honey, and bring to a simmer, about 5 minutes. (To make ahead, refrigerate in an airtight container for up to 2 days.)

Pour about half of the sauce into the large bowl with the dry spices, and stir until combined. (Reserve the remaining sauce in the pan.) Add the chicken wings and toss until the wings are evenly coated with the sauce.

Spread the chicken wings in a single layer on the prepared baking sheets. Be sure that the chicken wings have enough space between them to brown well on all sides. Bake for 25 minutes, then flip the wings, and bake for 25 minutes more, until the wings are cooked through and well browned.

Reheat the remaining sauce over medium heat until bubbling, 4 to 5 minutes. Transfer to a large bowl. Add the hot wings to the bowl and toss until the wings are well coated with the sauce. Serve warm or at room temperature.

(To make ahead, refrigerate the baked wings for up to 3 days. To reheat, spread the chilled wings on a foil-lined baking sheet and bake in a 300°F/150°C oven for about 10 minutes.)

EDITOR'S BEER CHOICE
Refreshing, slightly malty amber ale.

PICKLED VEGETABLES

Makes **about 3 cups/450 g**

1 cup/120 g cauliflower florets

2 large carrots, peeled, cut into ¼-in/6-mm slices

12 radishes, cut into ¼-in/6-mm slices

1 small red onion, cut into ¼-in/6-mm slices

2 jalapeño chiles, coarsely chopped

1½ cups/360 ml apple cider vinegar

1½ cups/360 ml water

1 tbsp coriander seeds

2 tsp peppercorns

2 bay leaves

¾ cup/150 g sugar

1 tbsp kosher salt

2 garlic cloves, peeled

1 tsp cloves

1½ tsp red pepper flakes

Pickles don't have to be a big project. It takes just a few minutes to make the brine and assemble the vegetables for this quick recipe; there's no canning required. Simply put them in a jar in the refrigerator and they'll keep for up to a month. They're an essential part of my Vegetarian Muffuletta, and in fact, they go with just about any sandwich. Sometimes I'll put a few in a bowl to serve with cocktails and a plate of sliced salami.

Layer the cauliflower, carrots, radishes, onion, and jalapeños in a clean 1-qt/960-ml glass jar with a tight-fitting lid. (You can substitute several smaller jars or a glass bowl.)

In a large saucepan, combine the vinegar, water, coriander seeds, peppercorns, bay leaves, sugar, salt, garlic, and cloves and bring to a boil. Stir occasionally, until the sugar and salt dissolve. Remove from the heat and add the red pepper flakes. Pour the liquid over the vegetables.

Cover and refrigerate overnight. Drain and serve at room temperature.

(To make ahead, store in an airtight container for up to 1 month.)

OKRA PEPERONATA

Serves **6**

1 lb/455 g okra, trimmed

3 tbsp olive oil

1 large red onion, halved and sliced

Kosher salt

2 red bell peppers, seeded and sliced into ¼-in/6-mm strips

2 yellow or orange bell peppers, seeded and sliced into ¼-in/6-mm strips

1¼ lb/570 g tomatoes, seeded and chopped

2 garlic cloves, minced

1 tsp fresh thyme

1 tsp fresh oregano

1 tsp sweet paprika

¼ tsp cayenne pepper

⅓ cup/75 ml water

1 tbsp finely chopped fresh basil leaves

2 tbsp balsamic vinegar

Freshly ground black pepper

For this updated dish of stewed okra and tomatoes, I look to Southern Italy for bell peppers and onion along with some fresh herbs and balsamic vinegar. This mixture makes a great vegetarian main course served with grits cakes or an accompaniment to smoked meats. When shopping, look for small okra pods. They're ideal for this dish.

If the okra pods are small, leave them whole; otherwise cut into 1-in/2.5-cm pieces.

In a wide sauté pan, heat 2 tbsp of the oil over medium-high heat until shimmering. Add the onion and a pinch of salt and cook, stirring occasionally, until the onions start to brown, about 8 minutes. Add the remaining 1 tbsp oil, the okra, red and yellow bell peppers, and a pinch of salt and cook, stirring occasionally, until the peppers soften and the vegetables start to brown, 10 to 15 minutes.

Add the tomatoes, garlic, thyme, oregano, paprika, cayenne, and water. Cover partially and bring to a simmer. Reduce the heat to medium and cook, stirring occasionally, until the vegetables are tender, about 10 minutes. Uncover the pan, stir in the basil and vinegar, and cook for about 30 seconds more. Season with salt and pepper. Serve immediately.

JERK CHICKEN WITH FRESH PINEAPPLE SALSA

Active **1 hr**; Total **1 hr 30 min plus 4 hr marinating**; Serves **4**

At Brown Sugar Kitchen, Tanya Holland cooks this not-too-spicy jerk chicken in the wood-smoked barbecue until it emerges juicy and crisp. The pineapple salsa she serves alongside is great to make ahead; it gets tastier as it sits overnight.

1. Make the marinade Combine all of the ingredients with ½ cup of water in a medium bowl.

2. Make the rub Combine all of the ingredients with 2 teaspoons of salt and ½ teaspoon of black pepper in a small bowl.

3. Coat the chicken with the spice rub and place in a 9-by-13-inch baking dish. Pour the marinade over the chicken and turn to coat. Cover and refrigerate for at least 4 hours and up to 24 hours.

4. Make the habanero vinegar In a blender, puree the habanero with the vinegar.

5. Make the pineapple salsa Combine all of the ingredients in a medium bowl.

6. Remove the chicken from the marinade, letting the excess drip off. Transfer the chicken to a baking sheet and let come to room temperature, about 30 minutes.

7. Light a grill or heat a grill pan. Brush the chicken all over with the habanero vinegar. Grill the chicken over moderately high heat, turning often, for 30 to 35 minutes, until the skin is nicely charred and an instant-read thermometer inserted in the thickest parts reads 165°F. Let the chicken rest for 5 minutes. Serve with the pineapple salsa.

JERK MARINADE

- 1 red onion, thinly sliced
- ¾ cup soy sauce
- ¾ cup vegetable oil
- ½ cup apple cider vinegar
- 1 jalapeño, sliced

JERK SPICE RUB

- 1 tablespoon garlic powder
- 1 tablespoon onion powder
- 1½ teaspoons ground allspice
- 1 teaspoon each freshly grated nutmeg, cascabel or ancho chile powder, cinnamon and cayenne pepper
- Kosher salt and black pepper

- One 4- to 5-pound chicken, cut into 8 pieces

HABANERO VINEGAR

- ½ habanero chile, stemmed and seeded
- ⅓ cup white wine vinegar

PINEAPPLE SALSA

- ½ pineapple—peeled, cored and finely diced (about 2 cups)
- 1 small red onion, finely diced (about ½ cup)
- 3 small jalapeños, finely diced
- ⅓ cup finely diced red bell pepper
- ⅓ cup chopped cilantro
- 2 tablespoons canola oil
- 2 tablespoons fresh lime juice
- Kosher salt

EDITOR'S WINE CHOICE
Fruit-forward, robust, dry rosé.

FOR MORE ON TANYA HOLLAND
tanyaholland.com
🅕 Tanya Holland
🐦 @tanyaholland

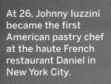

At 26, Johnny Iuzzini became the first American pastry chef at the haute French restaurant Daniel in New York City.

SUGAR RUSH

Master Tips, Techniques & Recipes for Sweet Baking

BY JOHNNY IUZZINI WITH WES MARTIN

Pastry superstar Johnny Iuzzini has worked in the world's most exalted kitchens, mentored by French chefs like Daniel Boulud and Jean-Georges Vongerichten. In his latest book, the former club kid uses his training to create thrilling recipes that reflect his global influences: "Nothing, except maybe a ride on a track on my Ducati, is more exciting than pulling together flavors and textures that make people flip," he writes. He starts with step-by-step instructions for fundamentals like custards and caramels, then moves on to the next level of complexity and creativity. He transforms a simple meringue into vanilla, berry and espresso marshmallows, and rejiggers a basic cake recipe into spicy, amped-up brownies (p. 118). Iuzzini proves to be the best kind of teacher, building confidence, then letting readers "take off the training wheels and have some fun."

Published by Clarkson Potter, $40

KILLER CHOCOLATE CHIP COOKIES

Makes **about 4 dozen 2-inch cookies**

½ **pound (2 sticks) cold unsalted butter, diced (226 g)**

1 **cup granulated sugar (200 g)**

1 **cup (packed) light brown sugar (232 g)**

¾ **teaspoon vanilla extract (4 g)**

¼ **teaspoon almond extract**

1 **large egg**

2 **large egg yolks**

2 **cups all-purpose flour (250 g)**

1 **cup cake flour (110 g)**

1 **teaspoon baking powder (4 g)**

1 **teaspoon baking soda (6 g)**

½ **teaspoon ground cinnamon (1 g)**

1½ **teaspoons kosher salt (6 g)**

14 **ounces bittersweet chocolate (70% cacao), coarsely chopped (397 g)**

Maldon sea salt (smoked, if you can find it), for garnish

People constantly ask me how I stay thin working as a pastry chef. While I do love sugar, I am able to restrain myself around most desserts. Cookie dough, though, is the devil, and baking it into these crunchy cookies, which are great for dunking in milk, doesn't help much either. They have a fine crumb and crisp texture, due to the addition of cake flour, and have a more intriguing flavor from a good hit of kosher salt and a pinch of cinnamon. This recipe makes a big batch of dough, enough to share, even if you have willpower like mine.

Preheat the oven to 350°F. Line 2 baking sheets with silicone baking mats or parchment paper.

Put the butter, granulated sugar, and brown sugar into a standing mixer bowl and toss with your fingers until the butter is coated. Attach the bowl and paddle to the mixer and beat the butter and sugar on medium-low speed until a thick paste forms with no visible butter lumps. Add the vanilla and almond extracts and mix well. With the motor on low speed, add the egg and egg yolks, one at a time, mixing well between additions. Stop the mixer and scrape down the bowl with a rubber spatula.

Meanwhile, in a separate bowl, sift together the flours, baking powder, baking soda, and cinnamon; sprinkle the kosher salt over the top. With the mixer on low speed, slowly add the dry ingredients to the butter mixture, stopping frequently to scrape down the bowl. Mix until just combined; remove the bowl from the mixer and fold the chocolate into the dough by hand.

Using a small (½-ounce) ice cream scoop, scoop level balls of dough and arrange them about 2 inches apart on the lined cookie sheets. Use the bottom of a glass to flatten the dough balls slightly and then sprinkle a little Maldon salt over each cookie. Bake for 12 to 13 minutes, rotating the pans once, until just set and the bottoms are beginning to brown. Cool for 10 minutes on the pans before transferring to a rack to cool completely.

Store the cookies in an airtight container for up to 3 days. If they last that long.

NOTE

This dough freezes well, either in bulk, which can be defrosted, scooped, and baked, or prescooped and shaped into balls that you can just put on a lined baking sheet and bake whenever you are craving them, adding another minute or two to the baking time.

SPICY MALTED CHOCOLATE CHIPOTLE BROWNIES

Makes **about 2 dozen 2-inch-square brownies**

½ pound (2 sticks) unsalted butter, plus more for the pan (226 g)

2 to 3 tablespoons Demerara sugar, for the pan

10 ounces bittersweet chocolate (66 to 72% cacao), chopped (284 g)

2 ounces unsweetened chocolate, chopped (57 g)

3 tablespoons barley malt syrup (75 g)

4 large eggs

2 cups granulated sugar (400 g)

2 teaspoons vanilla extract (10 g)

1½ cups all-purpose flour (190 g)

1 teaspoon baking powder (4 g)

1½ teaspoons chipotle chile powder (3 g)

1½ teaspoons smoked paprika (3 g)

¾ teaspoon cayenne pepper (1 g)

1 teaspoon kosher salt (4 g)

This decadent brownie is not for the faint of heart—this is a bar with an attitude. It is dense, intense, and has a one-two punch of heat from chipotle and paprika powders. The earthy richness of the malt gives the brownies almost a fermented flavor; the heat and the maltiness linger long after you finish one. A little bite goes a long way.

Preheat the oven to 350°F. Butter an 8 x 11-inch baking dish or cake pan and coat it generously with Demerara sugar, tapping out the excess.

Put the bittersweet and unsweetened chocolate and the ½ pound butter into a large heatproof bowl. Fill a saucepan one-third full of water and bring it to a simmer. Set the bowl over the simmering water, making sure the bottom of the bowl does not touch the water. Stir the chocolate occasionally until completely melted. Remove from the heat, stir in the malt syrup, and cool to room temperature.

Put the eggs, granulated sugar, and vanilla into a standing mixer bowl and set it over the simmering water, making sure the bowl does not touch the water. Whisk constantly until the sugar has dissolved and the mixture is hot to the touch (180°F). Transfer the bowl to the mixer, attach the whisk, and whip on high speed until pale, fluffy, and cooled to room temperature, about 10 minutes.

Meanwhile, sift together the flour, baking powder, chile powder, paprika, and cayenne into a bowl; sprinkle the salt on top. With a large, flat rubber spatula, fold the whipped egg mixture into the cooled chocolate until just combined but still streaky. Sprinkle the dry ingredients in 4 additions over the chocolate, folding until just combined between additions.

Transfer the batter to the prepared pan and smooth the top with the spatula. Bake in the center of the oven for about 50 minutes, until a toothpick or cake tester comes out clean.

Cool the brownies completely in the pan before cutting into 2-inch squares.

CRUMB CAKE

Makes **one 9 x 13-inch cake**; Serves **12 to 16**

FOR THE CAKE

Vegetable oil cooking spray

2 cups all-purpose flour, plus more for the pan (250 g)

5⅓ tablespoons (⅓ cup) unsalted butter, at room temperature (75 g)

½ cup granulated sugar (100 g)

1 large egg, at room temperature

¼ cup sour cream, at room temperature (60 g)

⅔ cup whole milk, at room temperature (160 g)

1 tablespoon vanilla extract (15 g)

1 tablespoon baking powder (12 g)

Pinch of kosher salt

FOR THE CRUMB TOPPING

2¼ cups all-purpose flour (280 g)

1¼ cups (packed) light brown sugar (290 g)

1 tablespoon ground cinnamon (6 g)

½ pound (2 sticks) unsalted butter, melted (226 g)

Confectioners' sugar, for dusting

During my tenure as pastry chef at four-star Restaurant Daniel, I had a group of very special interns every Saturday, who were lovingly referred to as "Johnny's Angels." One of the angels was Martha Magliula, who is an avid home baker extraordinaire. Every Saturday she would bring two coffee cakes—one for the team and one just for me. I had to ration it to get me through until the next Saturday. When I decided to do a cookbook focused on home bakers, I knew I just had to feature her incredible coffee cake, which doesn't skimp on the crumble topping.

To make the cake, preheat the oven to 350°F. Spray a 9 x 13-inch glass baking dish with cooking spray, dust it with flour, and tap out the excess.

Beat the butter and granulated sugar in a standing mixer fitted with the paddle on medium speed until lightened. Add the egg and sour cream and mix well.

Meanwhile, stir the milk and vanilla together. Sift together the 2 cups flour and the baking powder into a small bowl and sprinkle the salt on top.

With the mixer on low speed, alternately add the dry and wet ingredients to the bowl, beginning and ending with the dry. Stop the mixer several times to scrape down the bowl with a rubber spatula; mix until just combined. Transfer the batter to the baking dish and spread it evenly with an offset spatula.

To make the topping, whisk the flour, brown sugar, and cinnamon together in a bowl until well mixed. Add the melted butter and stir until the dry ingredients are thoroughly moistened. Using your hands, gently roll the mixture together between your palms and fingers until very small balls form; scatter the topping evenly over the cake batter in the pan right from your hands as you roll.

Bake the cake on the center rack of the oven for about 30 minutes, until the center is firm to the touch and springs back lightly. If the cake is not baked through, reduce the temperature to 325°F and continue baking in 5-minute increments until the cake is set in the center but the topping does not get too brown.

Dust the surface of the cake lightly with confectioners' sugar and cool completely on a rack. Once cool, dust the surface generously with confectioners' sugar before cutting and serving.

SWEET POTATO CUSTARD (CLAFOUTIS)

Active **20 min;** Total **1 hour 20 min;** Serves **8**

Softened butter, for greasing the pan

1 large sweet potato, peeled and cut into 1-inch pieces, or 1 cup store-bought sweet potato puree

1⅓ cups packed light brown sugar

⅓ cup all-purpose flour

1½ teaspoons kosher salt

1 teaspoon cinnamon

½ teaspoon ground mace

½ teaspoon ground cardamom

½ teaspoon ground cloves

8 large eggs

¾ cup whole milk

¾ cup heavy cream

2½ teaspoons pure vanilla extract

½ cup hazelnuts—toasted, skinned and coarsely chopped (see Note)

Confectioners' sugar, for serving (optional)

"Sweet potatoes work nicely in dessert," Johnny Iuzzini says. "They're low in starch and inherently high in sugar, with a pudding-like texture when cooked correctly." He blends sweet potato puree into a batter for clafoutis, a classic French custard tart. "The clafoutis will puff up in the oven but settle back into the pan, with a light fluffy texture like a good pumpkin pie."

1. Preheat the oven to 350°F. Grease an 8-by-11-inch glass baking dish with butter.

2. If using fresh sweet potato, bring 1 inch of water to a boil in a steamer. Add the sweet potato and cook until very soft, about 15 minutes. Drain very well. Transfer to a food processor and puree until smooth. Let cool.

3. In a small bowl, whisk the brown sugar, flour, salt, cinnamon, mace, cardamom and cloves. In a stand mixer fitted with the whisk or in a large bowl using a handheld mixer, whisk the eggs, milk and cream at low speed. Gradually beat in the sugar mixture, scraping down the side of the bowl as necessary. Add the sweet potato puree and vanilla and mix until combined.

4. Scrape the batter into the prepared dish and bake in the center of the oven for 20 minutes. Rotate the dish and sprinkle the hazelnuts evenly on top. Bake for 20 to 25 minutes longer, until the custard is set and a cake tester inserted in the center comes out clean. Transfer to a rack and let cool. Serve slightly warm or at room temperature, sprinkled with confectioners' sugar, if desired.

MAKE AHEAD The baked custard can be refrigerated for up to 1 day. Rewarm before serving.

NOTE To toast and skin hazelnuts, spread the nuts in a pie plate and toast in a 350°F oven until golden and the skins blister, about 12 minutes. Let cool slightly, then transfer to a clean kitchen towel and rub off the skins.

FOR MORE ON JOHNNY IUZZINI
johnnyiuzzini.com
 Chef Johnny Iuzzini
 @Johnny_Iuzzini

Ikarians enjoy plant-based meals drawn from the island's abundant produce. Above, the author's friend dries figs, an important staple in the local diet.

IKARIA

Lessons on Food, Life & Longevity from the
Greek Island Where People Forget to Die

BY DIANE KOCHILAS

Author Diane Kochilas dramatically calls Ikaria "the Greek island where people forget to die." She links the extraordinary longevity and good health of the locals to their diet of lean, plant-based dishes—"the Mediterranean diet of half a century ago." Kochilas, who grew up spending summers on Ikaria and now runs a cooking school there with her husband, shares delicious recipes from this inspiring place. These include familiar Greek dishes like hortopita, a crispy phyllo pie overflowing with leafy greens, zucchini and handfuls of herbs (p. 126), as well as more obscure island specialties like a Swiss chard soup ingeniously thickened with cornmeal (p. 124). Kochilas points out another reason Ikarians live so long: a laid-back attitude toward punctuality. Clocks on the island are largely irrelevant: "A running joke, when you ask someone what time it is, is to answer *argamisi,* or 'late-thirty.'"

Published by Rodale, $35

CORNMEAL & GREENS SOUP

Tsorvas

Makes **6 servings**

6 tablespoons Greek extra-virgin olive oil

2 red onions, finely chopped (about 2 cups)

2 garlic cloves, smashed with the side of a knife

1 pound (450 g) Swiss chard, coarsely chopped

1 cup coarsely chopped fresh mint leaves

1 cup coarsely chopped fresh chervil

6 cups (or more) water or low-sodium chicken broth or vegetable broth

1 cup polenta (coarse cornmeal)

Sea salt and freshly ground black pepper

Crumbled goat's milk cheese or Greek feta cheese, for garnish (optional)

I have been hearing about tsorvas *and the use of corn kernels and cornmeal in the Ikarian diet ever since my Aunt Mary, who passed away several years ago at the age of 97, mentioned the corn-stuffed cabbage leaves she remembered as a child. Other nonagenarians have talked to me about* tsorvas, *which was either some kind of cream (akin to polenta) or soup, or pilaf made with either the dried, milled corn kernels of a sweet white corn that is still grown on the island, or with a meal or flour made with the same corn. I have never been able to find either an exact definition or an exact recipe, so I tried my best to approximate what* tsorvas *was in the recipe below. Whatever it was exactly, corn was an important part of the diet before the advent of rice and it was one of the major foods of sustenance. It's also quite delicious!*

In a large, wide soup pot, heat 3 tablespoons of the olive oil over medium-low heat. Add the onions and garlic and cook until wilted, about 5 minutes.

Add the chard and half the herbs to the mixture and stir until wilted. Add 4 cups of the water or broth, bring to a boil, and in a slow, steady stream add the cornmeal, stirring vigorously with a wooden spoon all the while. Season to taste with salt and pepper.

Add the remaining 2 cups water (or broth) and simmer the soup until thick and creamy, about 30 minutes total. About 5 minutes before removing from the heat, add the remaining herbs and, if necessary, additional water or broth to maintain the soup's liquid, creamy consistency.

Drizzle in the remaining 3 tablespoons olive oil just before serving. If desired, garnish the soup with a little crumbled cheese.

SUMMER GREENS PIE WITH ZUCCHINI & HERBS

Hortopita Kalokairini

Makes **8 to 10 servings**

3 pounds (1.5 kg) zucchini, preferably large, coarsely grated

Salt and freshly ground black pepper

½ cup plus 5 tablespoons Greek extra-virgin olive oil, plus more for oiling the pan

3 large red onions, finely chopped

½ pound (250 g) amaranth leaves (if available) or Swiss chard, chopped

5 to 10 squash blossoms (if available), cleaned of pistils and finely chopped

2 cups finely chopped wild fennel (see Author's Note)

1 cup chopped fresh mint leaves

1 cup chopped fresh flat-leaf parsley

Leaves from 1 bunch fresh oregano, finely chopped

1½ cups crumbled Greek feta cheese

Basic Homemade Phyllo Dough, at room temperature (see Editor's Note)

Flour or cornstarch, for rolling out the phyllo dough

AUTHOR'S NOTE

If you can't get wild fennel, substitute 1 large fennel bulb, finely chopped, and 1 cup snipped dill. Add the fennel bulb when you cook the onions. Add the dill when you add the mint and parsley.

Zucchini, which grows in copious amounts in so many Ikarian gardens, is put to good use in many dishes, but by far this savory pie, an icon of summer on the island, is one of my personal favorites. A similar pie, but with pumpkin instead of zucchini, is made in the fall. This pie is delicious: It's herbaceous, sweet from the onions, and earthy from the flavor of the greens.

Place the zucchini in a colander and toss with salt. Place a plate over the zucchini and a weight, such as cans, over the plate. Let the zucchini drain for 1 to 3 hours, or overnight. Squeeze bunches at a time in your hands to get as much liquid as possible out. It is important for the zucchini to be as dry as possible. Place in a large bowl.

Position a rack in the center of the oven and preheat to 375°F (180°C). Lightly oil a 15-inch (39.5-cm) round baking or paella pan or a shallow, rectangular roasting pan or rimmed baking sheet (16 x 12-inch [40 x 30 cm]).

In a large skillet, heat 2 tablespoons of the olive oil over medium heat. Add the onions and cook until soft, about 10 minutes. Add the zucchini and cook over low heat until it releases any remaining liquid. Add the amaranth (or Swiss chard) and cook down so that the greens also release their liquid and it evaporates. If there is still residual liquid in the pot, drain the vegetables in a colander for a few minutes. Transfer the onion-zucchini-greens mixture to a large bowl and combine with the squash blossoms (if using), herbs, and feta. Season to taste with salt and pepper and mix in 3 tablespoons of olive oil.

Divide the phyllo dough into 4 equal-size balls. On a lightly floured surface, roll out the first dough ball, using the shape of your pan as the guide. For round pans, roll out to a round about 18 inches in diameter; for rectangular pans, roll out to a rectangle about 3 inches larger than the perimeter of the pan. Place the dough inside, leaving about 2 inches (5 cm) hanging over the edge. Brush with 2 tablespoons of olive oil. Repeat with the second piece of dough. Brush that, too, with olive oil.

Spread the filling evenly inside the pan, over the second layer of phyllo.

Repeat the rolling process for the third sheet, placing it over the filling, and pressing down gently. Brush generously with olive oil.

Finally, roll out the last piece of dough to a slightly smaller piece and place it over the surface of the pie. Join and fold in the bottom and top overhanging dough, rolling it decoratively around the perimeter of the rim. Brush the top of the pie generously with olive oil. Score the top of the pie into serving pieces, taking care to not draw the knife all the way through to the bottom of the pan.

Bake until the pastry is golden and crisp and the pie pulls away from the edges of the pan, 40 to 50 minutes. Remove, cool in the pan, and serve.

SPINACH RICE

Spanakorizo

Makes **4 servings**

4 tablespoons Greek extra-virgin olive oil

1 cup finely chopped red onion

1 garlic clove, minced

1 cup long-grain rice

8 cups chopped fresh spinach, about 1 pound (450 g), stems removed, cleaned well

½ cup water

½ cup chopped wild fennel fronds or dill

Sea salt and freshly ground black pepper

Juice of 2 lemons, strained

Spinach rice is still one of the classics of the Greek table, on Ikaria and all over the country. But rice was not always plentiful. Older recipes for this dish call for bulgur instead, which may be substituted in this and other pilafs.

In a large heavy skillet, heat 2 tablespoons of the olive oil over medium heat. Add the onion and cook, stirring frequently, until soft, 2 to 3 minutes. Stir in the garlic. Add the rice and stir with a wooden spoon over medium-low heat for 3 minutes.

Add the spinach, cover, and cook until the spinach loses most of its volume. Add the water, fennel (or dill), and salt and pepper to taste. Simmer, covered, stirring occasionally until all the liquid is absorbed and the rice is cooked and very tender, 25 to 30 minutes. Add more water as needed if you think it is necessary to achieve a creamy consistency. You can do so about halfway into cooking the mixture. Add the lemon juice 3 minutes before the end.

POTATOES BRAISED WITH WILD FENNEL

Patatato

Makes **4 servings**

8 scallions, chopped

6 tablespoons Greek extra-virgin olive oil

6 medium Yukon Gold potatoes, peeled and cut into 1½-inch (4-cm) cubes

½ cup white wine

Sea salt and freshly ground black pepper

1 cup chopped wild fennel or fennel fronds

Juice of 1 lemon

Patatato *on other Greek islands such as Amorgos is a meat and potato stew. When researching recipes for this book, I came across this dish, which is meatless, and cooked it one spring day as we were enjoying our annual Easter break on the island. I thought I had unearthed something old and unique, until my husband walked in the door, looked in the pot, and said, "Oh,* patatato. *I haven't seen that in a long time!" It is very common.* Patatato *is about as simple as simple gets, but the freshness of ingredients and the intense flavor of wild fennel make it uncannily sophisticated.*

In a large, wide pot, combine the scallions and 3 tablespoons of the olive oil. Cover and cook over low heat until the scallions are soft and translucent, about 7 minutes.

Add the potatoes, wine, and enough water just to come about halfway up the contents of the pot. Season with sea salt to taste. Cover and simmer until the potatoes are almost cooked, about 25 minutes.

Add the wild fennel and a bit more water if necessary to keep the mixture moist. Cover and continue simmering until the potatoes are fork-tender, another 10 to 15 minutes. Just before serving, stir in the lemon juice, remaining 3 tablespoons olive oil, and pepper to taste. Serve hot or at room temperature.

PORK & COLLARD GREEN STEW

Hoirino Mageiremeno me Lahanides

Makes **4 to 6 servings**

2/3 cup Greek extra-virgin olive oil

2¼ pounds (1 kg) bone-in pork shoulder or leg, cut into serving-size pieces

Salt and freshly ground black pepper

2 large red onions, chopped (about 2 cups)

2 tablespoons all-purpose flour

1 cup dry white wine

1 to 2 cups water or stock

3 pounds (1.5 kg) collard greens, trimmed and cut into ribbons 1½ inches (4 cm) wide

Juice of 1 to 2 lemons (to taste)

Pork and cabbage is a globally loved combination of flavors, and this dish is essentially a version of that, since collards are in the cabbage family. This lemony pork and collard stew is probably the most popular winter recipe on Ikaria, a Sunday and Christmas treat that calls for strong wine and company. There are at least three versions of this dish. The first, below, is with fresh pork, preferably bone-in (for more flavor). But the more traditional versions, if you have a family pig and a fireplace over which to smoke it once you slaughter it, are for smoked pork. The leg is usually smoked, but I've also come across this recipe made with smoked pancetta, which you can find in Italian markets.

In the recipe below the pork and collards are finished with a thick, lemony sauce, which helps balance the richness of the pork and the almost musky, cabbagy flavor of the collards. If you can't find collards, you can use bok choy (Chinese cabbage). This dish is usually served with roasted potatoes.

In a large wide pot, heat the olive oil over medium-high heat. Add the pork, in batches if necessary, and sear, turning with kitchen tongs to brown on all sides. Season with salt and pepper.

Push the pork to one side of the pot and add the onions. Reduce the heat to medium and cook, stirring the onions occasionally, until soft and translucent, 8 to 10 minutes. Sprinkle the flour into the pot. Mix gently to combine with the onions and pork. Cook for 2 to 3 minutes.

Pour in the wine. When the alcohol sizzles off, add enough water (or stock) to come about halfway up the height of the meat. Cover, reduce the heat to low, and simmer until the meat is tender but not completely done, 1 hour to 1 hour 15 minutes.

Add the collards to the pot. Mix in gently. Season again with salt and pepper. Cover and cook until the greens and meat are both very tender and the meat is falling off the bone, another 35 to 40 minutes. About 5 minutes before removing from the heat, pour in half the lemon juice, taste it, and pour in the rest if desired. Remove from the heat and serve.

EDITOR'S WINE CHOICE
Cherry-rich, medium-bodied red Côtes du Rhône.

WILD RICE WITH SPICED GREEK CAULIFLOWER, CLEMENTINES & HAZELNUTS

Active **35 min**; Total **1 hr**; Serves **4**

- 1 cup wild rice
- ¼ cup toasted hazelnuts
- 3 tablespoons extra-virgin olive oil, plus more for drizzling
- 2 large red onions, coarsely chopped
- 2 large garlic cloves, finely chopped
- 1 medium head of cauliflower, cut into small florets (6 cups)
- 6 drained oil-packed sun-dried tomatoes, chopped
- 2 rosemary sprigs
- ½ teaspoon ground cumin
- ½ teaspoon ground turmeric

  Kosher salt and pepper
- 2 clementines or mandarin oranges, peeled and separated into sections

EDITOR'S WINE CHOICE
Lively, lemony Greek white.

Diane Kochilas simmers cauliflower and onions with cumin and antioxidant-rich turmeric, which turns the vegetables a brilliant yellow. She adds a bit of crunch to the dish with earthy wild rice, but you can also swap in farfalle pasta.

1. In a large saucepan of salted boiling water, cook the wild rice until tender, 45 to 50 minutes. Drain well.

2. Grind the hazelnuts in a mini food processor until finely ground.

3. In a large skillet, heat the 3 tablespoons of olive oil over moderate heat. Add the onions and cook, stirring often, until softened, 8 to 10 minutes. Add the garlic and cook, stirring, until fragrant, about 30 seconds. Add the cauliflower, sun-dried tomatoes, rosemary, cumin and turmeric. Season with salt and pepper and toss. Add ½ cup of water, cover and cook, stirring occasionally, until the cauliflower is just tender, 7 to 9 minutes. Discard the rosemary sprigs.

4. Stir the clementines into the cauliflower and cook until heated through, about 3 minutes. In a large bowl, toss the wild rice with the cauliflower. Garnish with the ground hazelnuts and a drizzle of olive oil and serve.

FOR MORE ON DIANE KOCHILAS
dianekochilas.com
Diane Kochilas
@DianeKochilas

Erin Patinkin (left) met Agatha Kulaga
at a book club; a year later, the two
self-taught bakers opened Ovenly.

OVENLY

Sweet & Salty Recipes from New York's Most Creative Bakery

BY AGATHA KULAGA & ERIN PATINKIN

Adding a sprinkling of salted breadcrumbs to apple quick bread (p. 134), or bananas and a swirl of Nutella to coffee cake (p. 138): These are the kinds of brilliantly simple ideas that have earned the Brooklyn bakery Ovenly a cult following. Before finding a permanent home for Ovenly, co-owners Erin Patinkin and Agatha Kulaga slept in their beat-up delivery van (nicknamed "Wedgie") and woke up at 3 a.m. to borrow a local pizza oven—all in the service of their exceptional, not-too-sweet, sometimes vegan baked goods. In their debut book, the duo are generous not only with their recipes but with their hard-won baking insights, offering step-by-step instructions with photographs to explain tricky techniques like latticing pie crust (equal-size pieces are easier to weave) and browning butter.

Published by Harlequin, $30

SALTED APPLE BREAD

Yield **one 9 x 5-inch loaf**

Softened unsalted butter
and flour, for preparing
the loaf pan

½ cup (4 ounces) unsalted
butter

¾ cup whole milk

¾ cup sugar

2 large eggs, at room
temperature

¼ cup maple syrup (the darker
the better; we use Grade B)

¼ cup hazelnut oil (or
substitute ¼ cup canola oil)

½ teaspoon vanilla extract

2 cups all-purpose flour

1 cup rolled oats

½ cup whole-wheat pastry flour

1½ teaspoons ground cinnamon

1 teaspoon baking soda

1 teaspoon baking powder

1 teaspoon salt

¼ teaspoon ground cloves

¼ teaspoon ground nutmeg

1½ cups (7 ounces) peeled,
cored and cubed (into
½-inch pieces) apples

Salted Breadcrumb Topping
(recipe follows)

After making our Thanksgiving pies last year, we found ourselves overwhelmed with tons of extra apples, so we decided to cut them into chunks and freeze them for other recipes, like this one. The Salted Breadcrumb Topping adds a bit of savory to this lightly sweetened batter.

1. Preheat the oven to 375°F. Grease a 9 x 5-inch loaf pan with softened butter and dust the pan with flour.

2. In a small saucepan over low heat (or in a small, microwave-safe bowl in a microwave oven), melt the butter and set aside to cool.

3. In a large bowl, whisk together the whole milk, sugar, eggs, maple syrup, oil, vanilla extract and melted butter until well blended.

4. In a separate large bowl, whisk together the all-purpose flour, oats, whole-wheat pastry flour, cinnamon, baking soda, baking powder, salt, cloves and nutmeg.

5. Using a spatula or a wooden spoon, add the flour-oat mixture to the milk mixture until almost combined. Fold in the apples until the ingredients are just wet, and the fruit is distributed throughout the batter.

6. Pour the batter into the prepared loaf pan and top with the Salted Breadcrumb Topping.

7. Bake for 50 to 55 minutes, or until a toothpick inserted in the center of the bread comes out clean.

Salted Breadcrumb Topping

Yield **topping for one loaf**

1 tablespoon unsalted butter

½ cup breadcrumbs,
homemade or store-bought

½ teaspoon salt

1. In a small saucepan, melt the butter over medium-low heat.

2. Add the breadcrumbs and salt, and stir continuously until the breadcrumbs are golden and fragrant, 5 to 7 minutes.

JELLY DOUGHNUT MUFFINS

Yield **12 muffins**

Softened unsalted butter
or nonstick cooking spray or
12 baking cups, for greasing
or lining the muffin tin

2 cups all-purpose flour

1½ teaspoons baking powder

1 teaspoon ground nutmeg

1 teaspoon ground cinnamon

½ teaspoon salt

¾ cup sugar

¼ cup canola oil

1 large egg, at room
temperature

¾ cup whole milk

¼ cup plus 2 tablespoons jam
of your choice, for filling

¼ cup (4 tablespoons) unsalted
butter, for brushing

⅓ cup sugar

1 tablespoon ground cinnamon

When we were craving doughnuts but making muffins, we realized that the in-between was a cinnamon-sugar batter filled with our homemade blueberry jam. A doughnut, but a muffin, too!

1. Preheat the oven to 350°F. Grease the wells of a 12-cup muffin tin with softened butter or nonstick cooking spray, or use baking cups.

2. In a medium bowl, whisk together the flour, baking powder, spices and salt. Set aside.

3. In a large bowl, whisk together the sugar, canola oil and egg. Add the whole milk and whisk until smooth.

4. Add the flour mixture to the egg mixture and stir with a spatula until just combined.

5. Using a scoop or a spoon, fill each muffin tin well with 2 tablespoons of batter (you can eyeball it). Spoon 1½ teaspoons jam onto the very center of the batter (it should not touch the sides of the muffin tin well), and then top with another 2 tablespoons of batter. Repeat until all the wells have been filled.

6. Bake for 22 to 24 minutes, or until a toothpick inserted in the center of a few muffins comes out clean.

7. Five minutes before the muffins are done baking, in a small saucepan over low heat or in a small, microwave-safe bowl in a microwave oven, melt the butter and set aside to cool. In a small bowl, combine the sugar and cinnamon. Set aside.

8. Remove the muffins from the oven and let cool for 5 minutes. Dip the top of each warm muffin into the melted butter, and then lightly dip it into the cinnamon sugar topping, coating each muffin evenly.

9. Let cool and serve.

BANANA NUTELLA COFFEE CAKE

Yield **one 13 x 9-inch cake, cut into 12 pieces**

Softened unsalted butter and all-purpose flour, for preparing the baking pan

CAKE

1 **cup (16 tablespoons, 8 ounces) unsalted butter**

3¾ **cups all-purpose flour**

2 **cups sugar**

1 **tablespoon baking powder**

1½ **teaspoons salt**

¼ **teaspoon baking soda**

1 **cup buttermilk**

4 **large eggs, at room temperature**

¼ **cup sour cream (preferably full-fat)**

2 **teaspoons vanilla extract**

FILLING

2 **small ripe bananas, peeled and thinly sliced**

½ **cup Nutella, or another hazelnut-chocolate spread**

¼ **cup (packed) light brown sugar**

TOPPING

Coffee Cake Streusel (recipe follows)

We love the classic combination of sweet bananas and creamy Nutella for coffee cake filling. Nutella retains its consistency when baked inside a dough or batter, so it looks beautiful when the cake is sliced.

1. Preheat the oven to 350°F. Grease a 13 x 9-inch baking pan with softened butter and dust the pan with flour.

2. In a small saucepan over low heat (or in a small, microwave-safe bowl in a microwave oven), melt the butter and set aside to cool.

3. In a large bowl, whisk together the flour, sugar, baking powder, salt and baking soda.

4. In a separate large bowl, whisk together the buttermilk, eggs, sour cream, vanilla extract and melted butter until very smooth.

5. Using a spatula or a wooden spoon, mix the dry ingredients into the wet ingredients until combined.

6. Layer half of the batter in the prepared baking pan, smoothing it out to the edges and leveling the top. This batter is thick, so evenly spoon or scoop it in tablespoon-size mounds into the pan before spreading. Use the back of a spoon or an offset spatula (this works best) to smooth it in the pan.

7. Spread the banana slices evenly over the batter, overlapping the slices. Drizzle the Nutella over the bananas (if it's too thick, melt it in a small saucepan over very low heat, or in a small, microwave-safe bowl in a microwave oven for 15 seconds). Sprinkle with the light brown sugar.

8. Layer the remaining batter over the filling using the same method of spooning or scooping. Smooth out the top of the batter, ensuring it is even and reaches the edges of the pan.

9. Sprinkle the top with streusel, and then bake for 50 to 55 minutes, or until a toothpick inserted in the center of the cake comes out clean.

continued on p. 140

BANANA NUTELLA COFFEE CAKE *continued*

Coffee Cake Streusel

Yield **streusel for 1 coffee cake**

4 tablespoons (2 ounces) unsalted butter

1 cup all-purpose flour

3 tablespoons sugar

2 tablespoons (packed) light brown sugar

1¼ teaspoons ground ginger

1 teaspoon ground cinnamon

We developed this streusel specifically for our coffee cakes. Drier than what you might put on a cobbler or a pie, it adds a nice crunch. It's great for topping sweet quick breads, too.

1. In a small saucepan over low heat (or in a small, microwave-safe bowl in a microwave oven), melt the butter and set aside to cool.

2. In a medium bowl, whisk the remaining ingredients, breaking up the brown sugar and distributing it throughout the mixture (using your hands works well here, too).

3. Add the melted butter to the flour-spice mixture and mix with a fork or a wooden spoon until fully incorporated and clumps form (again, you can mix with your hands, which is our preferred method).

4. Unbaked streusel keeps in an airtight container in the freezer for up to 1 month.

CHOCOLATE CHEESECAKE WITH SOUR CREAM TOPPING

Yield **one 8-inch cake**

CRUST

6 **tablespoons (3 ounces) unsalted butter**

2 **tablespoons sugar**

1½ **cups finely ground graham cracker crumbs (about 12 graham crackers, pulverized in a food processor or by hand)**

FILLING

2 **cups (two 8-ounce packages) cream cheese, softened**

1¼ **cups sugar**

½ **cup unsweetened Dutch-process cocoa powder**

2 **large eggs, at room temperature**

1 **teaspoon vanilla extract**

Pinch of salt

TOPPING

½ **cup sour cream (full-fat or plain full-fat yogurt), at room temperature**

2 **tablespoons sugar**

½ **teaspoon vanilla extract**

Pinch of salt

Just like our recipes, Erin and I are the perfect partnership of sweet and savory. This airy, tangy and chocolaty cheesecake recipe was passed on to us by Mama Patinkin and reflects this balance. Erin says this was her all-time favorite dessert growing up, and she still loves it. The first time we made this cake together, I got hooked, too.

1. Prepare the crust. In a small saucepan over low heat (or in a small, microwave-safe bowl in a microwave oven), melt the butter and set aside to cool. Pour the butter into a large bowl and whisk in the sugar and then the graham cracker crumbs. Combine thoroughly.

2. Press the graham cracker mixture into the bottom of an 8-inch springform pan and a third of the way up the sides. Freeze the crust for at least 30 minutes to set.

3. Preheat the oven to 375°F.

4. Prepare the filling. Beat the cream cheese in the bowl of a standing mixer fitted with a paddle attachment (or using a hand mixer) on medium speed, until fluffy, about 2 minutes. Turn the machine off, scrape down the sides of the bowl, and add 1¼ cups sugar and the cocoa. Mix on low for 10 seconds. Increase the speed to medium-high and beat until smooth, about 1 minute.

5. Scrape down the sides of the bowl, and with the machine off, add the eggs, vanilla extract and salt. Beat the filling on medium-low speed for about 10 seconds, then increase the speed to medium-high until fluffy and silky smooth, about 30 more seconds.

continued on p. 142

CHOCOLATE CHEESECAKE
WITH SOUR CREAM TOPPING *continued*

6. Remove the prepared crust from the freezer, and pour the filling into the springform pan. Smooth the top with a spatula, and bake for 30 minutes.

7. While the cheesecake bakes, prepare the topping. In a large bowl, whisk together the sour cream, sugar, vanilla extract and salt.

8. Remove the cheesecake from the oven, leaving the oven at 375°F. Very carefully spoon the sour cream topping on the hot cake, and use a spatula to smooth it to form a thin, even layer over the top, being careful not to press too hard on the delicate, hot cake. Return the cheesecake to the oven, and bake for 30 to 40 minutes more, or until the top looks set.

9. Cool the cheesecake completely at room temperature, and then chill it thoroughly (for at least 6 hours) before serving.

GINGER MOLASSES COOKIES

Total 30 min plus cooling; Makes 1 dozen cookies

2 cups all-purpose flour

4½ teaspoons ground ginger

2 teaspoons baking soda

1 teaspoon natural unsweetened cocoa powder

1 teaspoon cinnamon

½ teaspoon ground cardamom

½ teaspoon freshly ground black pepper

½ teaspoon fine sea salt

¾ cup granulated sugar

¼ cup packed light brown sugar

⅔ cup canola oil

1 large egg

¼ cup unsulfured molasses

½ cup crystallized ginger, cut into ¼-inch dice

½ cup turbinado sugar, such as Sugar in the Raw

"Out of all of the seasonal cookies at Ovenly, we love this one the most," Erin Patinkin says. The cookies have a phenomenal crumbly-crisp texture with chewy bits of candied ginger inside and a crackly dusting of turbinado sugar outside. Patinkin and Ovenly partner Agatha Kulaga like to sandwich the oversize cookies with buttercream or stir pieces into ice cream.

1. Preheat the oven to 350°F. In a medium bowl, whisk the flour with the ground ginger, baking soda, cocoa powder, cinnamon, cardamom, pepper and salt. In a large bowl, whisk the granulated and brown sugar with the oil, egg and molasses. Add the dry ingredients and crystallized ginger and stir until just combined.

2. Scrape the dough out onto a work surface and pat into a thick disk. Cut the disk into 12 wedges and roll each wedge into a ball. Place the turbinado sugar in a small bowl and roll each ball of dough in the sugar to coat evenly. Arrange the balls 3 inches apart on 2 baking sheets lined with parchment paper.

3. Bake the cookies for 8 to 10 minutes, until just set at the edges; rotate the sheets from top to bottom and front to back halfway through baking. Let the cookies cool for 10 minutes, then transfer them to a rack and let cool completely.

FOR MORE ON AGATHA KULAGA & ERIN PATINKIN

oven.ly

Ⓕ Ovenly

🐦 @Ovenly

TEENY'S TOUR OF PIE

A Cookbook

BY TEENY LAMOTHE

When her Sunday tradition of baking a pie became the highlight of her week, Chicago-based actress Teeny Lamothe decided to open a pie shop. But first, she needed to master pie baking. In her cookbook, she details her year of "total pie immersion" as she explored America and apprenticed for established "lady pie bakers." She writes, "I wanted to study under strong women who'd had the gumption to open their own shops, in the hopes that one day I might be like them." Lamothe reveals her Five Commandments of Crust, delves into regional classics (including Southern favorites like chess pie) and shares recipes of her own invention, like her delicately sweetened and salted Bourbon Bacon Pecan Pie (p. 146). The recipes are so compelling you'll want to follow Lamothe's advice about the book: "Smear it with butter, dust it with flour, stain it with berry juice and, most of all, make a lot of pie."

Published by Workman, $16

BOURBON BACON PECAN PIE

Prep **30 min** • Bake **50 to 60 min** • Total **1 hr 30 min** • Makes **one 9-inch single-crust pie (6 to 8 slices) or four 5-inch single-crust pies**

Pecan pie has never been my favorite. More often than not it's too sugary and too heavy and the lovely nutty, salty goodness of the pecans is often smashed out of existence by the cloying sweetness of the corn syrup. Every Thanksgiving I barely make it through half a slice before waving the white flag of surrender. Somewhere in the wake of half-eaten, disappointing slices I realized that, as a pie baker, I could make a change. I had the ability to reimagine pecan pie in a way that made it palatable to my sugar-sensitive taste buds.

I started by experimenting with different types of sugar and the quantity in which I used them. The amount of corn syrup I used needed to stay the same because any less and the filling became crumbly as opposed to custardy under the quintessential candied sugar layer. So I tested and tinkered with various sugars—white, dark brown and light—until I hit upon a winner. By the time I was finished I felt like the Goldilocks of pecan pie; light brown sugar was just right.

At that point I had a pretty stellar but altogether traditional pecan pie recipe. A few somethings were missing; I just didn't know what those somethings were yet. While I was looking at a million different recipes to get the proportions right, Google kept mentioning that people often put bourbon into their pecan pies. Having grown up in the company of fairly conservative, "by the Betty Crocker book" bakers, I'd never heard of liquor in a pie. As an adult, however, I'd developed a pretty serious crush on bourbon; I was certainly willing to give it a try. Unsurprisingly, I loved it. The hint of bourbon played nicely with the pecans, and the first few bites had me smiling with delight...but the "sweet" was still too emphatic. I realized, at this point, I was on the lookout for something salty.

That's when my bacon wheels started turning. One day I crumbled a few strips into my filling, and the result was out of this world. Bourbon Bacon Pecan Pie is good. It's slap-you-in-the-face-and-then-eat-a-second-slice good. It's the coming together of diverse but delicious ingredients to create the ultimate super-tasty pie.

continued on p. 148

BOURBON BACON PECAN PIE *continued*

6 tablespoons (¾ stick)
unsalted butter, at room
temperature

1 cup packed light brown sugar

3 large eggs

½ teaspoon salt

1 teaspoon pure vanilla extract

¾ cup dark corn syrup

2 tablespoons bourbon

4 strips bacon, well cooked and
roughly chopped

1½ cups chopped pecans

1 disk dough from Whole
Wheat Crust (recipe follows)

Up to 3 tablespoons all-
purpose flour, for rolling out
the crust

There are people who have questioned this union, confused and cautious, having already formed a strong opinion about whether or not bacon belongs in a pie. They are easily won over. Others recognize right away the greatness of combining bourbon, bacon, and pecans. They are usually on their second slice by the time the doubters realize how much they like what they are eating. Between the two, Bourbon Bacon Pecan Pie rarely lasts longer than an evening. Slowly but surely I've won people over, and Bourbon Bacon Pecan Pie has become one of my signature recipes.

1. Preheat the oven to 350°F with a rack in the middle position.

2. Whisk together the butter and sugar with a wire whisk in a large mixing bowl until the mixture is light and fluffy. Add the eggs, one at a time, mixing after each addition. Add the salt, vanilla, corn syrup, and bourbon and whisk until everything is fully incorporated. Stir in the bacon and 1 cup of the chopped pecans. Set aside.

3. Prepare the crust: Place the dough on a floured work surface and with a floured rolling pin roll it into a rough 11-inch circle about ⅛ inch thick. Lay the crust into a 9-inch pie dish, gently press it in, and trim any excess dough from the edge with a paring knife, being sure to leave a ¾-inch overhang. Tuck the overhanging dough under itself and crimp. Place the lined pie dish on a rimmed baking sheet.

4. Arrange the remaining ½ cup of pecans in a layer on the bottom of the pie shell. Give the filling one last stir, in case anything has settled to the bottom. Pour the filling over the pecans and bake until the crust and the pecans are golden brown and the middle of the pie no longer wobbles, 50 to 60 minutes. Let cool at room temperature until the filling is set, at least 45 minutes, before serving.

Bourbon Bacon Pecan Pie will keep for 4 to 5 days, covered, on the countertop.

Whole Wheat Crust

Prep **15 min** · Chill **1 hr, ideally overnight** · Total **1 hr 15 min** · Makes **one 9-inch double crust, four 5-inch double crusts, or eight 5-inch single crusts**

1½ cups all-purpose flour

1 cup white whole wheat or whole wheat flour

2 teaspoons salt

2 tablespoons granulated sugar

¾ cup (1½ sticks) cold unsalted butter, cut into small pieces

¼ cup (4 tablespoons) cold vegetable shortening

¼ cup (4 tablespoons) cold vodka

½ cup (8 tablespoons) cold water, plus extra as needed

Whole wheat crust is my go-to for nearly every pie I bake. Whole wheat flour is slightly more challenging to work with because of its low gluten content, but adding vodka to the mix makes for a wonderful, workable dough. I keep my (cheap) vodka in the freezer and the chill of it serves to cool down the rest of my ingredients as I mix the dough together. If you have made pie crust before, you might wonder about the amount of liquid I call for here; I have found that whole wheat flour requires a little more liquid to come together into a ball of dough.

This recipe makes enough dough for a nine-inch top and a bottom crust. If you need only a bottom crust, you can freeze half of this recipe for up to 3 months and save it for later.

1. In a large bowl, stir together the flour, salt, and sugar until everything is thoroughly combined. Add the butter and shortening and cut the mixture together using a pastry cutter until it forms small pea-size crumbs coated in flour.

2. Pour the vodka evenly over the dry ingredients, a few tablespoons at a time, using a rubber spatula to press the dough together. Similarly, add the water, and continue to press the dough together to form a large ball. The dough should be fairly wet and sticky; if for some reason it seems particularly dry, add a little extra ice water a tablespoon at a time until everything comes together easily. (Be careful to work the dough as little as possible; otherwise the crust may be tough.)

3. Divide the dough into two equal balls, press each into a disk, wrap each in plastic, and refrigerate for at least an hour or up to 2 days before rolling out.

MY MOM'S RHUBARB STRAWBERRY CUSTARD PIE

Prep **30 min** • Bake **55 min** • Total **1 hr 30 min** • Makes **one 9-inch double-crust pie (6 to 8 slices)**

1 cup hulled, sliced strawberries (sliced about ¼ inch thick)

4 cups diced rhubarb (from 3 to 4 stalks (see Author's Note)

1½ cups granulated sugar

5 tablespoons all-purpose flour, plus extra for rolling out the crust

2 large eggs

2 disks dough from Buttery All-Purpose Crust (recipe follows)

AUTHOR'S NOTE

When buying rhubarb, look for firm, thick stalks with healthy leaves. Trim off and discard the leaves (they're mildly poisonous!) and chop the stalks crosswise as you would celery.

This lattice pie is one of my mom's summertime favorites. We grew our own strawberries and rhubarb, so at the earliest sign of having enough of each, my mom would head to the backyard to pick them. Most strawberry rhubarb pies have the strawberries front and center while the rhubarb takes a backseat to its sweeter counterpart, but this pie does the opposite. The rhubarb is the spotlight ingredient with just a hint of strawberry and a simple custard-like filling to help temper the rhubarb's acidity. When I was growing up, I couldn't comprehend how my mom actually enjoyed the unique flavor rhubarb has to offer, let alone make an entire pie out of it. My brother and I clamored endlessly for her famous tart cherry pie, but in between the constant cherry demands she would bake one of these pies...and she wouldn't share a slice. Now that I've been swayed to her way of thinking, I beg her to bake these— and I make her share.

1. Preheat the oven to 450°F with a rack in the middle position.

2. Place the strawberries and rhubarb in a large bowl and toss gently to combine.

3. Whisk together the sugar and flour in a small bowl. Add the eggs and whisk until the mixture is smooth. Set aside.

4. Prepare the bottom crust: Place one disk of the dough on a lightly floured surface and with a floured rolling pin roll it into a rough 11-inch circle about ⅛ inch thick. Lay the crust into a 9-inch pie plate, gently press it in, and trim any excess dough from the edge with a paring knife, being sure to leave a ¾-inch overhang.

5. Place the strawberries and rhubarb in the crust. Give the egg mixture another stir and pour it evenly over the fruit.

6. Prepare the lattice crust: On a floured work surface with a floured rolling pin, roll out the remaining dough disk into an 11-inch circle about ⅛ inch thick. Cut the dough into strips and weave them into a lattice. Tuck the overhanging dough strips under the bottom crust and crimp together, pressing to seal.

7. Set the pie on a rimmed baking sheet and bake for 10 minutes, then reduce the heat to 325°F and bake until the crust is golden brown, an additional 45 minutes. Allow the pie to cool and set before serving.

My Mom's Rhubarb Strawberry Custard Pie will keep for 3 to 4 days, covered, on the countertop.

Buttery All-Purpose Crust

Prep **15 min** · Chill **1 hr** · Total **1 hr 15 min** · Makes **one 9-inch double crust or four 5-inch double crusts**

2½ cups all-purpose flour

2 teaspoons salt

2 tablespoons granulated sugar

¾ cup (1½ sticks) cold unsalted butter, cut into 1-inch pieces

¼ cup (4 tablespoons) cold vegetable shortening

¼ cup (4 tablespoons) cold vodka

6 tablespoons cold water, plus extra as needed

Sometimes I'm just not in the mood for a whole wheat crust. Either I think it's going to compete with the flavors that I'm using in the filling, or I'm just feeling slightly less nutty (ha!) and want a crust made with only all-purpose flour. I decided to develop my own all-purpose-flour recipe because as much as I like my mom's recipe, I love the richness that butter adds. My mom's recipe is wonderfully flaky, whereas this recipe is slightly more decadent because of the butter. It's fairly similar to my recipe for Whole Wheat Crust; it simply calls for less liquid.

I find that whole wheat flour needs a little more moisture than all-purpose in order to come together nicely, so I've adjusted this recipe accordingly. This recipe yields a double crust; if you want to make only enough dough for a single crust, simply halve the recipe (or make the whole batch and freeze half).

1. In a large bowl mix together the flour, salt, and sugar until everything is thoroughly combined. Add the butter and shortening and cut the mixture together using a pastry cutter until it forms small pea-size crumbs coated in flour.

2. Pour the vodka over the dry ingredients a few tablespoons at a time while using a rubber spatula to press the dough together. Similarly, add the water, and continue to press the dough together to form a large ball. The dough should be fairly wet and sticky; if for some reason it seems particularly dry, add a little extra ice water a tablespoon at a time until everything comes together easily. (Be careful to work the dough as little as possible, otherwise the crust may be tough.)

3. Divide the dough into two equal balls, press each into a 1-inch disk, wrap each in plastic, and refrigerate for at least 1 hour or up to 2 days before rolling out.

COCONUT CREAM PIE

Prep **30 min** · Chill **4 hr** · Total **4 hr 30 min** · Makes **one 9-inch single-crust pie (6 to 8 slices) or four 5-inch single-crust teeny pies**

½ cup granulated sugar

3 tablespoons packed cornstarch

½ teaspoon salt

2 cups whole milk

4 large egg yolks

2 tablespoons unsalted butter

1 teaspoon pure vanilla extract

1 cup sweetened shredded coconut flakes

1 prebaked 9-inch Buttery All-Purpose Crust (p. 151; see Editor's Note)

Homemade whipped cream, for serving

EDITOR'S NOTE

Directions for prebaking: Place the dough in the pie plate; prick the bottom and sides with a fork. Freeze the pie plate until the dough is firm, about 20 minutes. Meanwhile, preheat the oven to 350°F. Line the dough with parchment or foil, pressing it along the sides. Fill the lining with dried beans or pie weights and bake until the crust is set, about 15 minutes. Remove the lining and weights, then continue to bake until the crust is golden brown, about 10 minutes. Transfer the crust to a wire rack and let cool.

Not being a big cream-pie-making sort of family meant that when we went out to a restaurant that happened to have coconut cream on the menu, I was guaranteed to order it. Cream pies were a special restaurant treat and coconut cream was always my favorite. I'm a coconut lover. Scattered all over my kitchen are tiny canning jars filled to the brim with toasted coconut. Why? Because I happen to think it's the perfect snack. And to this day, if I see coconut cream on the menu I'm tempted to order it. But I usually refrain because I know that if I wait, and make it at home, I'll get all the extra toasted coconut to myself.

1. Combine the sugar, cornstarch, and salt in a medium saucepan and whisk together. Add the milk and egg yolks and whisk together until there are no lumps.

2. Place the saucepan over medium heat and cook, whisking constantly, until the mixture comes to a low simmer and begins to thicken, about 7 minutes. Continue cooking, whisking constantly and being sure to scrape the bottom of the pan to prevent scorching, until the mixture begins to boil, about 2 minutes. Still whisking constantly, let it boil for a full minute, then immediately remove it from the heat.

3. Add the butter and vanilla, whisking until the butter has melted and the mixture is smooth. Add ¾ cup of the coconut and stir with a spoon to fully incorporate.

4. Pour the coconut cream into the prebaked pie crust and, while still hot, cover it with plastic wrap to prevent a film from forming on the top. Refrigerate until the cream has set, at least 4 hours.

5. While the cream is setting (at least 30 minutes before you wish to serve the pie), preheat the oven to 350°F.

6. Spread the remaining coconut on a rimmed baking sheet and toast, flipping halfway through with a spatula, until it is light brown, 7 to 10 minutes. Remove the coconut from the oven and let cool for a few minutes.

7. Remove the plastic wrap from the pie, top with the whipped cream, and sprinkle with the toasted coconut. Serve cold.

Coconut Cream Pie will keep for 2 to 3 days, covered, in the refrigerator.

ESPRESSO FRENCH SILK PIE WITH BLACKBERRY COMPOTE

Prep **25 min** · Chill **4 hr** · Total **4 hr 25 min** · Makes **one 9-inch single crust pie (6 to 8 slices) or four 5-inch single-crust teeny pies**

¾ cup (1½ sticks) unsalted butter, at room temperature

1 cup granulated sugar

3 ounces unsweetened chocolate, melted and cooled

3 tablespoons freshly brewed espresso, at room temperature

½ teaspoon pure vanilla extract

3 pasteurized large eggs (see Author's Note)

1 prebaked 9-inch Graham Cracker Crust (recipe follows)

Homemade whipped cream, for topping

Blackberry Compote (recipe follows), for serving

AUTHOR'S NOTE
This recipe calls for raw eggs. Unpasteurized eggs may contain harmful bacteria, so please make sure you use pasteurized eggs. They are available at most supermarkets.

When I was little I would beg my mom to put a few spoonfuls of her coffee into my hot chocolate so I could be a lady and drink a "mocha." This pie reminds me of that, the way the light and fluffy chocolate is piled high and topped with whipped cream with just a hint of espresso to surprise your taste buds. (Since I don't have an espresso maker, I go to my local coffee shop and ask for a shot of espresso to go.)

This pie is similar to the more traditional French silk, but here the espresso and blackberries lend some unexpected twists. In a manner similar to layering strawberries into the bottom of a traditional French silk pie, I like to spoon a sweet blackberry compote over the slices of this one when serving. It reminds me of my time in Seattle, where I was surrounded by coffee and blackberries at every turn.

1. Cream together the butter and sugar in the bowl of a stand mixer fitted with the paddle attachment, or in a large bowl using a handheld electric mixer, on medium-high speed until it is light and fluffy, about 4 minutes.

2. Scrape down the side of the bowl with a rubber spatula and add the melted chocolate. Mix on high until the mixture is very fluffy, 5 minutes. While the mixer is still running add the espresso and vanilla and continue to mix for another minute.

3. Turn the speed down to medium and add the eggs, one at a time, beating for 3 minutes after each addition. After the addition of the third egg the mixture should be lighter in color and smoother and silkier in texture.

4. Spoon the filling into the cooled graham cracker crust, smooth the top with a spatula, and refrigerate, uncovered, for at least 4 hours. Before serving, top with the whipped cream and serve cold with the blackberry compote on top or alongside.

Espresso French Silk Pie will keep for 3 to 4 days, covered, in the refrigerator.

continued on p. 156

ESPRESSO FRENCH SILK PIE continued

Graham Cracker Crust

Prep **10 min** • Bake **5 to 7 min** • Total **20 min** • Makes **one 9-inch single crust or four 5-inch single crusts**

1½ **cups graham cracker crumbs (from 8 to 9 graham cracker sheets; see Author's Note)**

2 **tablespoons granulated sugar**

6 **tablespoons (¾ stick) unsalted butter, melted**

AUTHOR'S NOTE

To make the graham cracker crumbs, pulse the crackers in a food processor until they form very fine crumbs, or seal them in a large ziplock bag and crush them with a rolling pin or the palm of your hand.

1. Preheat the oven to 350°F with a rack in the middle position.

2. Whisk together the graham cracker crumbs and the sugar in a medium bowl to combine. Pour the melted butter over the crumbs and mix with a spoon or a rubber spatula until the butter is evenly distributed. The graham mixture will be slightly darker and should clump easily when pressed together.

3. Spoon three quarters of the mixture into a 9-inch pie plate and, using your fingers, press the mixture up along the side of the plate until you have a ¼-inch-thick shell all the way around. Spoon the rest of the mixture into the center of the plate and press it to form the bottom of the shell, making sure the bottom and sides are joined.

4. Bake until the shell is slightly browned, 5 to 7 minutes. Remove it from the oven and let it cool on a rack before filling.

Blackberry Compote

Makes **about 2 cups**

¼ **cup granulated sugar**

Pinch of ground cinnamon

2 **tablespoons cornstarch**

About 1 teaspoon brewed espresso, at room temperature (optional)

1½ **cups fresh or frozen blackberries**

When I found myself hopelessly lost in Seattle I comforted myself with wild blackberries, and soon after that I realized I wanted to add them to everything. Their tantalizing tart yet sweet flavor is a perfect match for the subtle espresso notes featured in this light-as-air chocolate pie.

1. Whisk together the sugar, cinnamon, and cornstarch in a small bowl. Add ½ cup water and the espresso, if using, and whisk until smooth.

2. Place the blackberries in a medium saucepan, add the sugar mixture, and cook over medium-low heat, stirring often to prevent scorching, until the berries thicken enough to coat the back of a spoon, 7 to 10 minutes. Let the mixture come to a boil and cook, stirring occasionally, for 1 minute, then remove the pan from the heat.

3. Let the compote cool completely before using it to top the individual slices of pie.

Blackberry Compote will keep for 1 week, covered, in the refrigerator.

ROASTED CORN & TOMATO TARTS

Active **30 min**; Total **2 hr 15 min**; Serves **4 to 6**

2 cups cherry tomatoes, halved

1 cup fresh corn kernels

½ medium red onion, finely diced

1 garlic clove, thinly sliced

1 tablespoon extra-virgin olive oil

¼ teaspoon kosher salt

Pepper

1 recipe Whole Wheat Crust dough (p. 149)

¼ pound fresh mozzarella, thinly sliced

2 tablespoons finely chopped basil

EDITOR'S WINE CHOICE

Ripe, intensely fruity, dry California rosé.

Teeny Lamothe mounds corn kernels, cherry tomatoes and fresh mozzarella cheese in a flaky, buttery whole-wheat crust for these easy-to-form savory tarts. "The look you're going for by the end is a very rustic tart called a galette," Lamothe says.

1. Preheat the oven to 325°F. In a 9-by-13-inch baking dish, toss the cherry tomatoes with the corn, onion, garlic, olive oil and salt; season with pepper. Bake for 45 minutes, until the tomatoes have softened. Transfer the dish to a rack and let cool completely. Increase the oven temperature to 350°F.

2. Line a large rimmed baking sheet with parchment paper. Cut the dough in half. On a lightly floured work surface, roll each piece of dough into a 12-inch round and set them on the baking sheet (they will overlap slightly).

3. Mound half of the tomato-corn mixture in the center of each round, leaving a 1-inch border. Top the filling with the mozzarella and sprinkle with the basil. Fold up the edges of the tarts, pleating as you go. Both tarts should now fit on the baking sheet.

4. Bake the tarts for about 1 hour, until the crust is golden brown. Serve warm.

FOR MORE ON TEENY LAMOTHE

teenypies.com

❑ Teeny Pies

🐦 @teenypies

MY PARIS KITCHEN

Recipes & Stories

BY DAVID LEBOVITZ

David Lebovitz was the pastry chef at Chez Panisse in Berkeley when, for reasons he's never been able to articulate, he decided to move to Paris 11 years ago. Since then he's made a witty anthropological study of the local habits ("I have yet to attend a party in Paris where a bowl of cherry tomatoes wasn't offered") and created his own style of entertaining— chronicled on his superpopular blog and in this cookbook, his sixth. His recipes reflect how the French eat today, combining very classic dishes like chicken in a rich Dijon mustard sauce (p. 162) with Americanized ones like a butternut squash gratin topped with a cornmeal-sage crumble (p. 165): "The French have taken to *les crumbles*, baked dishes that Americans call crisps." Part insider, part outsider, he is most wholly himself as a host; his recipes and storytelling reveal the generous spirit of someone who, more than anything, loves inviting people into his kitchen.

Published by Ten Speed Press, $35

CHERRY TOMATO CROSTINI WITH HOMEMADE HERBED GOAT CHEESE

Tartines de Tomates Cerises, Chèvre Frais Maison aux Herbes

Serves **4**

HERBED FRESH GOAT CHEESE

- **2 cups (480 g) whole goats' (or cows') milk yogurt**
- **1 generous tablespoon very finely minced mixed fresh herbs (be sure to include chives, as well as an assortment that could include thyme, sage, basil, or flat-leaf parsley)**
- **1 tablespoon minced shallots**
- **1 teaspoon minced garlic**
- **¾ teaspoon sea salt or kosher salt**
- **Generous pinch of cayenne pepper**

ROASTED CHERRY TOMATOES

- **1½ pounds (680 g) cherry tomatoes, stemmed and halved**
- **3 tablespoons olive oil**
- **2 cloves garlic, peeled and thinly sliced**
- **Handful of fresh herbs (any combination of rosemary or thyme sprigs, bay leaf, and basil or sage leaves)**
- **Sea salt or kosher salt and freshly ground black pepper**

TOASTS

- **4 thick slices bread, such as ciabatta, a country bread, or a sourdough that's not too dense**
- **Olive oil**
- **1 clove garlic, peeled**

- **A few leaves of fresh basil, sage, or flat-leaf parsley, for garnish**

I like to roast the tomatoes ahead of time—up to 8 hours in advance—so they have time to marinate in their own savory juices, which caramelize slightly, making a nice bit of sauce to drizzle over the top.

1. To make the herbed goat cheese, line a mesh strainer with a few layers of cheesecloth or muslin and set it over a bowl. Scrape the yogurt into the lined strainer, fold the cloth over the yogurt, and refrigerate for 24 hours.

2. Put the strained yogurt into a bowl and mix in the herbs, shallots, garlic, salt, and cayenne pepper. Refrigerate until ready to use.

3. To roast the tomatoes, preheat the oven to 350°F (180°C). Combine the cherry tomatoes, olive oil, garlic, and herbs in a baking dish or pan that will hold them all in a snug single layer. Season with salt and pepper, mix well, and spread them out in the baking dish.

4. Roast the tomatoes for about 45 minutes, stirring once or perhaps twice during baking, until they're wilted and their juices are starting to concentrate—and perhaps brown a bit—in the bottom of the baking dish. Scrape the tomatoes and any juices into a bowl and let cool to room temperature. They can sit up to 8 hours, and they improve the longer they sit.

5. When ready to serve, make the toasts. Preheat the oven to 350°F (180°C). Evenly brush the bread slices with olive oil. Place them on a baking sheet and toast for about 5 minutes, until light golden brown. Remove from the oven and when just cool enough to handle, rub the slices generously with the garlic clove. Let cool to room temperature.

6. To serve, thickly smear each piece of toast with the fresh herbed cheese. Pluck out the herbs and spoon the tomatoes and their juices over the toasts. Coarsely chop the herbs for the garnish, and scatter them over the top of each portion.

CHICKEN WITH MUSTARD
Poulet à la Moutarde

Serves **4 to 6**

Many years ago, when prices were ridiculously low, I bought an enormous copper pan at E. Dehillerin, the famed cookware shop in Les Halles. This one-pan meal is a perfect fit for your largest, most extravagant pot. This dish requires you to brown the thighs and legs. Unless you have a very large skillet or a Dutch oven, fry the chicken in batches—you want them to have room to brown, not steam, which overcrowding creates.

- ½ cup (135 g), plus 3 tablespoons Dijon mustard
- ¼ teaspoon sweet or smoked paprika
- Freshly ground black pepper
- ¾ teaspoon sea salt or kosher salt
- 4 chicken thighs and 4 legs (8 pieces, total)
- 1 cup (100 g) diced smoked thick-cut bacon
- 1 small onion, peeled and finely diced
- 1 teaspoon fresh thyme leaves, or ½ teaspoon dried
- 1 cup (250 ml) white wine
- 1 tablespoon whole mustard seeds or grainy mustard
- 2 to 3 tablespoons crème fraîche or heavy cream
- Warm water (optional)
- Chopped fresh flat-leaf parsley or chives, for garnish

1. Mix ½ cup (135 g) of the Dijon mustard in a bowl with the paprika, a few generous grinds of the peppermill, and the salt. Toss the chicken pieces in the mustard mixture, lifting the skin and rubbing some of it underneath.

2. Heat a wide skillet with a cover or a Dutch oven over medium-high heat and add the bacon. Cook the bacon, stirring frequently, until it's cooked through and just starting to brown. Remove the bacon from the pan and drain on paper towels. Leave about 1 tablespoon of bacon fat in the pan, discarding the rest. Add the onion and cook for about 5 minutes, until soft and translucent. Stir in the thyme, and let cook for another few minutes, and then scrape the cooked onion into a bowl.

3. Add a little bit of olive oil to the pan, if necessary, and place the chicken pieces in the pan in a single layer. (If they don't all fit, cook them in two batches.) Cook over medium-high heat, browning them well on one side, then flip them over and brown them on the other side. It's important to get the chicken nicely colored as the coloring—as well as the darkened bits on the bottom of the pan, called the *fond*—will give the finished sauce its delicious flavor.

continued on p. 164

CHICKEN WITH MUSTARD continued

4. Remove the chicken pieces and put them in the bowl with the onions. Add the wine to the hot pan, scraping the darkened bits off the bottom with a sturdy flat utensil. Return the chicken pieces to the pan along with the bacon and onions. Cover and cook over low to medium heat, turning the chicken in the sauce a few times during cooking, until the chicken is cooked through, about 15 minutes. Check doneness by sticking a knife into the meat next to the thigh bone; if it's red, continue cooking for a few more minutes.

**EDITOR'S
WINE CHOICE**
Earthy,
concentrated red
Burgundy.

5. Remove the pot from the heat and stir in the 3 tablespoons Dijon mustard, the mustard seeds, and the crème fraîche. If the sauce has reduced and is quite thick, you can thin it with a little warm water. Sprinkle chopped parsley over the top and serve.

BUTTERNUT SQUASH CRUMBLE
Crumble de Butternut

Serves **6 to 8**

SQUASH FILLING

- **2 tablespoons salted or unsalted butter**
- **2 tablespoons olive oil**
- **4 pounds butternut squash (1.8 kg), peeled, seeded, and diced into ¾-inch (2-cm) cubes**
- **2 teaspoons minced fresh thyme leaves**
- **Sea salt or kosher salt and freshly ground black pepper**
- **½ cup (60 g) peeled and thinly sliced shallots**
- **1 cup (250 ml) chicken stock**
- **2 tablespoons finely chopped fresh flat-leaf parsley**

TOPPING

- **¾ cup (105 g) fresh or dried bread crumbs**
- **½ cup (70 g) stone-ground cornmeal or polenta**
- **½ cup (1½ ounces/45 g) freshly grated Parmesan cheese**
- **1 tablespoon minced fresh sage leaves**
- **1 teaspoon granulated sugar**
- **½ teaspoon sea salt or kosher salt**
- **4 tablespoons (2 ounces/55 g) unsalted butter, chilled and cubed**
- **1 large egg**

The French have taken to les crumbles, *baked dishes that Americans call* crisps. *This should not be confused with what the British call* crisps, *which are potato chips. Although I have some fond memories of long-simmered casseroles topped with shards of potato chips (or breakfast cereal), I think they'd be a tough sell with the French, so I stick with* crumble *so as not to confuse anyone around here, including me. (Thankfully, butternut, or* le butternut, *means the same thing in both languages.)*

This savory version of a crisp—er, I mean...crumble—is made with sage-scented bread crumbs with bits of crackly polenta to give it a crispy/crumbly texture.

1. Preheat the oven to 375°F (190°C). Generously butter a shallow 3-quart (3-liter) baking dish with softened butter.

2. To make the squash filling, heat 1 tablespoon of the butter and 1 tablespoon of the olive oil in a large skillet over medium-high heat. Add half of the squash and half of the thyme. Season with salt and pepper and sauté, stirring occasionally, until the squash pieces begin to brown on several sides.

3. Add half of the shallots and cook for another few minutes, until they're softened. Add ½ cup (125 ml) of the chicken stock and cook for about 30 seconds, stirring, to reduce the stock a bit and heat everything through. Scrape the squash mixture into the prepared baking dish.

4. Wipe the pan clean and heat the remaining 1 tablespoon of butter and 1 tablespoon of olive oil in the pan over medium-high heat. Cook the rest of the squash and thyme the same way, seasoning it with salt and pepper, and adding the remaining shallots and ½ cup (125 ml) of chicken stock, stirring. Scrape the cooked squash into the baking dish, stir in the parsley, then press the mixture into a relatively even layer. Cover the dish snugly with aluminum foil and bake for 30 minutes, until the squash is pretty soft when you poke it with a paring knife.

continued on p. 166

BUTTERNUT SQUASH CRUMBLE *continued*

5. While the squash is baking, make the topping by combining the bread crumbs, cornmeal, Parmesan, sage, sugar, and salt in the bowl of a food processor. Add the butter and pulse until the mixture is crumbly and the butter is completely incorporated. Add the egg and pulse a few more times until the mixture just starts clumping together in bits. (The topping can also be made by hand in a large bowl, using a pastry blender or your fingertips to mix in the butter and egg.)

6. Remove the squash from the oven, remove the foil, and cover with the topping. Decrease the oven temperature to 350°F (180°C) and return the dish to the oven. Bake for about 20 minutes, until the top is golden brown, and serve.

FOR MORE ON DAVID LEBOVITZ
davidlebovitz.com
David Lebovitz
@davidlebovitz

Every year, Renato Poliafito (left) and Matt Lewis celebrate the birthday of Baked, the bakery they opened in Brooklyn in 2005.

BAKED OCCASIONS

Desserts for Leisure Activities, Holidays & Informal Celebrations

BY MATT LEWIS & RENATO POLIAFITO

The most irreverent book yet from the geniuses behind New York City's Baked is a calendar of global holidays, from the major (Christmas) to the minor (Groundhog Day) to the not-quite-official-but-should-be (World Nutella Day). Between hilarious anecdotes—a particularly good one involves Renato Poliafito, age 11, in a Halloween costume that unintentionally makes him look like rocker Pat Benatar—the bakers have created a spectacular dessert resource. They celebrate classics in an apple-cranberry galette for Thanksgiving (p. 175) and brilliantly rethink retro desserts, as in the salted caramel soufflé they make for Julia Child's birthday (p. 172). Says Matt Lewis, "We would be thrilled if we could join together to make Dolly Parton's birthday a national holiday."

Published by Stewart, Tabori & Chang, $35

CHEESY BASTILLE DAY BEER BREAD

JUL 14 | Bastille Day
Yield **one 9-by-5-inch (23-by-12-cm) loaf • 12 servings**

4 ounces (115 g) Comté cheese, shredded

3 cups (385 g) all-purpose flour

1 tablespoon baking powder

1 teaspoon kosher salt

¼ teaspoon freshly ground black pepper

¼ teaspoon ancho chile powder (optional)

4 ounces (115 g) Pyrenees Brebis cheese or other semisoft sheep's-milk cheese, cut into ½-inch (12-mm) cubes

1¼ cups (10 ounces/300 ml) beer

1 large egg, beaten lightly

¼ cup (55 g) sour cream

2 tablespoons unsalted butter, melted

A fair number of Brooklynites are Francophiles at heart. And though the adoration for all things French (chic French, country French, coastal French) is not always bubbling on the surface, we have witnessed plenty of unironic beret-wearing hipsters sipping their morning lattes, scuffed Voltaire paperbacks in hand. Needless to say, Bastille Day is big in Brooklyn (and Manhattan). Despite its origin as the day the Bastille prison was stormed in 1789, which is considered to be the beginning of the French Revolution, here it is celebrated with a raucous, convivial, and charming street party. There are crepes and wine, éclairs and macarons, and lots and lots of cheese. It is one of the few foreign holidays so expertly co-opted and celebrated by New Yorkers that it almost feels...American.

As part-time Francophiles ourselves, we celebrate the day with loads of French cheese. Actually, we celebrate as many days as possible with as many cheeses as possible. But Bastille Day is a particularly great time to focus on and enjoy the cheeses of France. While we might occasionally indulge in the stinkier varieties, we are particularly obsessed with Comté these days. And when you pair that with a lovely sheep's-milk cheese from the Pyrenees region (we love Brebis) in a simple quick bread, you have the makings for a perfect cheesy loaf. The base of this recipe is the stalwart and omnipresent (at least in the 1980s) beer cheese bread. It is beyond simple—no yeast, no rising—and we did our best to make sure the flavors of the cheese shine. While, like all quick breads, this isn't as complex tasting as a sourdough, it is absurdly good as morning toast.

BAKED NOTE

We have been making cheesy quick breads for years, but the method of sprinkling the bottom of the pan with some cheese before baking was a revelation. Much credit to America's Test Kitchen for the brilliant idea; it adds a wonderful dimension: a crispy, cheesy top to an already wonderful bread.

1. Preheat the oven to 350°F (175°C) and position a rack in the center. Spray a 9-by-5-inch (23-by-12-cm) loaf pan with nonstick cooking spray.

2. Sprinkle approximately 1 ounce (30 g) of the Comté over the bottom of the pan in an even layer.

3. In a large bowl, whisk together the flour, baking powder, salt, black pepper, and the ancho chile powder, if using. Stir in the Brebis and 2 ounces (55 g) of the Comté, making sure each piece is completely coated in flour. Set aside.

4. In a medium bowl, whisk together the beer, egg, sour cream, and butter.

5. Add the wet ingredients to the flour mixture, using a rubber spatula to fold together until they are completely combined. Do not overmix.

6. Transfer the batter to the prepared pan. Smooth the top and sprinkle with the remaining 1 ounce (30 g) Comté. Bake, rotating the pan halfway through the baking time, until the top is browned and the loaf is cooked all the way through, 45 to 55 minutes; insert a toothpick into the center of the bread to check for doneness—it should come out clean (except perhaps for some melted cheese). Remove from the oven and place the loaf on a cooling rack for 20 minutes. Then turn it out onto a wire rack to cool completely.

7. Slice and serve; the bread can also be toasted before serving.

HOW TO STORE

The bread will keep, tightly wrapped, at room temperature for up to 2 days. It also freezes really well—wrap tightly in plastic wrap, then foil, before freezing.

SALTED CARAMEL SOUFFLÉ

AUG 15 | Julia Child's Birthday
Yield **8 decadent servings**

In June 2007 I rented (with family and friends) a small villa in the South of France just outside the perfectly picturesque town of Paradou. And in a way, I never left. In my mind's eye, I go back there often. Without warning, I am instantly in Paradou again. I am walking to town for warm baguettes and pain au chocolat. The bakery is thumbprint size and smells of butter. I am speaking halting (embarrassing) French with the pleasant town butcher. I am drinking magical wines on the magical grounds, with fig trees nearly smack up against a long, rectangular, insanely blue pool. And our entire group is reading the posthumously published autobiography of Julia Child, My Life in France, because it is a book about possibilities. For us, our little assembled vacationing group, Julia was not only the master of sole meunière; she was also about second chances and midlife career changes. After all, she didn't become Julia Child, chef and personality, until near her fiftieth birthday. Anything is possible.

When we think of Julia Child, rightly or wrongly, we think of soufflés (and Queen of Sheba cake—who can ever not think of the Queen of Sheba cake?). Soufflés are fluffy, and impressive, and decidedly French. Decidedly Julia. Our Salted Caramel Soufflé is a great way to celebrate Julia's birthday, and it is (if we do say so ourselves) a lot of fun to make. True, salted caramel is about as ubiquitous these days as water, but it is put to good use here. The soufflé is neither overly sweet nor overly salty, and the entire effect is one of subtle but sexy flavor; the telltale signs of sugar and smoke linger pleasantly. Happy birthday, Julia.

BAKED NOTE

Two important soufflé tips: First, make sure your eggs are really room temperature. We can't stress this enough. Avoid the temptation to hurry things along and use almost–room temperature eggs. Room-temperature egg whites whip up much more easily and provide more volume. Second, when we say fold, we really mean fold. Don't cheat and stir the egg whites into the caramel mixture—gently fold them. Slow and steady wins the race.

continued on p. 174

1½ cups (300 g) granulated sugar, plus more for the soufflé dish

1 tablespoon light corn syrup

½ cup (120 ml) heavy cream, at room temperature

2 teaspoons fleur de sel

1 cup (240 ml) whole milk

5 large egg yolks, at room temperature

3 tablespoons all-purpose flour

1 tablespoon cornstarch

6 large egg whites, at room temperature

¾ teaspoon cream of tartar

½ teaspoon kosher salt

Unsweetened whipped cream (optional)

SALTED CARAMEL SOUFFLÉ *continued*

1. Preheat the oven to 400°F (205°C) and position a rack in the lower third of the oven. Lightly butter the bottom and sides of a 2-quart (2-L) soufflé dish. Dust the soufflé dish with sugar (so that it adheres to the butter) and knock out the excess.

2. In a large saucepan with high sides, combine 1 cup (200 g) sugar, ¼ cup (60 ml) water, and the corn syrup. Stir the mixture gently so you don't splash any of it up the sides of the pan. Turn the heat to medium-high and continue stirring until the sugar dissolves. Increase the heat to high, stop stirring, clip on a candy thermometer (making sure the bulb is immersed in the sugar but not touching the pan), and allow the mixture to boil. Once it begins to turn a rich, dark caramel color and the thermometer reads 345°F (175°C), 5 to 8 minutes (don't worry if it takes longer, the actual time is reliant on so many factors), remove it from the heat; do not overcook. Gently and slowly stream in the heavy cream (it will bubble up, so be careful). Stir in the fleur de sel. Return the mixture to medium-low heat; don't worry if the caramel mixture begins to harden—it will easily melt again as it reheats. Add the milk and stir to combine. Reduce the heat to low. Leave the mixture on the heat while you prep the egg yolks.

3. In a large bowl, whisk together the egg yolks and ¼ cup (50 g) sugar. Sprinkle the mixture with the flour, then the cornstarch, and whisk until completely combined. Pour one-third of the caramel mixture into the egg mixture, whisking the egg mixture constantly. Slowly stream in the rest of the caramel while whisking constantly until combined. Set the bowl aside.

4. In the bowl of a standing mixer fitted with the whisk attachment (or using a whisk and bowl and a ready arm), whisk the egg whites on high speed for 1 minute. Sprinkle the cream of tartar and salt over the whites and continue whisking on high speed until the egg whites form soft peaks. Slowly stream in the remaining ¼ cup (50 g) sugar, and continue beating until stiff (but not dry) peaks form. Using a rubber spatula, gently fold one-quarter of the stiff egg-white mixture into the caramel mixture until almost combined. The caramel mixture will begin to lighten. Fold another quarter of the egg-white mixture into the caramel mixture until nearly combined. Finally, add the remaining egg-white mixture to the caramel mixture and fold gently until completely combined.

5. Transfer the soufflé batter to the prepared dish. For an even rise, run your thumb around the inside edge of the dish to wipe away any stray batter. Place the soufflé in the oven, and immediately reduce the oven temperature to 375°F (190°C). Avoid opening the oven door during the recommended baking time. Bake until the soufflé is puffy and dry to the touch, and the center is just about set but slightly jiggly (that is, slightly jiggly, not crazy ripply), 22 to 30 minutes.

6. Transfer the hot soufflé dish to a serving platter and serve immediately as is or with unsweetened whipped cream, if you like.

BROWN BUTTER APPLE CRANBERRY GALETTE

4TH THU IN NOV | Thanksgiving

Yield **one 10-by-14-inch (25-by-36-cm) galette • about 10 servings**

Try as we might, our respective Thanksgiving tables never look like the ones depicted in fancy food magazines. For starters, we don't own large Versailles-length tables, thousands of chairs, and acres of space. We each live in typical (space-challenged) Brooklyn apartments. More important, we don't have as much stuff as these magazine families. We don't have (i.e., we can't fit into our humble abodes) the place-card holders, the runners, the centerpieces, the endless china, the so-specific serving ware, and the various napkins. Who are these people who own an infinite supply of color-coordinated linens? Our Thanksgiving tables are simpler affairs. They have to be, and that is okay with us.

Our Brown Butter Apple Cranberry Galette happens to look stunning on a simple Thanksgiving table. In fact, it is so beautiful, it could be a centerpiece unto itself. Galettes, often described as rustic or hand-formed pies, might look intimidating, but they are actually easy to make. We filled ours, of course, with a bounty of typical Thanksgiving-inspired fare, a pleasing mix of apples and cranberries. And, like all good pies, the crust is also a star, super buttery and flaky. Our galette will definitely stand on its own on a Thanksgiving table, or you could just as easily serve it alongside the more typical pumpkin and pecan pies.

BAKED NOTE

Why do we use bread crumbs in this dessert? The bread crumbs help absorb some of the excess juice in the fruit filling, which results in an overall crisper galette. Also, if you don't have access to fresh cranberries (not in season or otherwise available), dried cranberries will work wonderfully, though the texture will be slightly chewier. Frozen cranberries are perfect as well, though be sure to thaw them first, and discard any liquid they may exude before tossing them with the apples. Finally, we rarely strain our brown butter; we like the mottled appearance it can give baked goods, and we think the slightly browned bits are the best part.

continued on p. 176

BROWN BUTTER APPLE CRANBERRY GALETTE *continued*

MAKE THE GALETTE DOUGH

1. Place the butter and shortening in a small bowl and freeze for at least 15 minutes and up to 30.

2. Add ¼ cup (60 ml) water to a measuring cup. Add a few ice cubes to the water to keep it cold, and place in the freezer for 15 minutes.

3. Place both flours, the sugar, and salt in a food processor and pulse until combined. Add the cold butter and shortening chunks. Pulse until the mixture is coarse and pebbly, with a few small chunks of butter and shortening still visible, 5 to 7 quick pulses. Remove the ice water from the freezer. Add 1 tablespoon ice water to the dough at a time, pulsing in between, until the mixture just starts to come together; it will likely take 3 to 4 tablespoons. Keep pulsing until a mass forms or until a pinch of dough in your fingers holds together. Turn the dough out onto a very lightly floured work surface and bring it together by kneading gently but briefly. Form the dough into a disk, wrap it tightly in plastic wrap, and refrigerate it for at least 1 hour or overnight.

MAKE THE SPICED APPLE FILLING

1. Peel and core the apples. Slice them into very thin (about ⅛-inch/ 3-mm) slices. Place the apples in a large bowl and toss together with the cranberries. Sprinkle the brown sugar, cinnamon, and salt over the fruit and toss again until the fruit is well coated and the mixture is combined.

2. Place the butter in a small saucepan over medium-high heat and cook, swirling the pan occasionally, until the foam subsides and the butter turns a light nut brown, 3 to 4 minutes; watch carefully so it does not burn. Remove from the heat and set aside to cool, about 5 minutes (pick up the pan and swirl it constantly to cool the butter more quickly). Remove 2 tablespoons of the butter to a small glass or mini prep bowl, then pour the remaining melted butter over the fruit mixture and toss with your hands to combine.

ASSEMBLE THE GALETTE

1. Place a 12-by-16-inch (30.5-by-40.5-cm) piece of parchment paper on a work surface and sprinkle it with a tiny bit of flour. Sprinkle the chilled dough with a little flour and place it on the parchment. Using a rolling pin, roll the dough out into a rough rectangle ⅛ to ¼ inch (3 to 6 mm) thick that covers or almost covers the parchment, sprinkling the dough with flour if necessary. Lift the parchment with the dough and place it inside a half sheet pan. Refrigerate the dough in the pan for about 15 minutes.

continued on p. 178

FOR THE GALETTE DOUGH

4 ounces (1 stick/115 g) cold unsalted butter, cut into ½-inch (12-mm) cubes

¼ cup (50 g) very cold vegetable shortening, cut into ½-inch (12-mm) cubes

Ice cubes

1½ cups (170 g) all-purpose flour, plus more for rolling out the dough

¾ cup (90 g) cake flour

2 tablespoons granulated sugar

1 teaspoon kosher salt

FOR THE SPICED APPLE FILLING

3 Granny Smith apples

½ cup (55 g) fresh cranberries, or dried (65 g), or frozen (60 g), thawed and drained (see Baked Note on p. 175)

¼ cup plus 2 tablespoons (85 g) firmly packed dark brown sugar

¼ teaspoon ground cinnamon

¼ teaspoon kosher salt

2 ounces (½ stick/55 g) unsalted butter

FOR THE ASSEMBLY

3 tablespoons very fine bread crumbs or panko

1 tablespoon sanding sugar

Vanilla ice cream (optional)

BROWN BUTTER APPLE CRANBERRY GALETTE *continued*

2. Preheat the oven to 400°F (205°C).

3. Remove the dough from the refrigerator and sprinkle the bread crumbs in the center of the dough, leaving a 2-inch (5-cm) empty border from the edge. Use your hands to lift the apples out of the bowl, shake them gently to remove excess liquid, and arrange decoratively (we like slightly overlapping concentric circles or a spiral pattern) over the bread crumbs, again keeping a 2-inch (5-cm) border all the way around. Next, use your hands to remove the cranberries from the bowl, leaving excess liquid behind (if using dried cranberries, give a slight squeeze to remove excess liquid), and arrange them in a circle in the center of the galette over the apples. Feel free to sprinkle the apples with a few tablespoons of the juice, but no more; discard any remaining liquid. Use the parchment paper to help turn the plain border of dough over the apples, using your fingers to pinch together any tears (much of the apple filling will be left exposed). Using a pastry brush, brush the reserved brown butter onto the dough and exposed apples. Sprinkle the dough and apples with the sanding sugar.

4. Bake for 35 to 45 minutes, until the crust is browned; try lifting the corner of the galette with a metal spatula—the bottom should be browned as well. (If the top of the galette crust or the fruit begins to brown too much before the galette is baked through, tent the top with foil for the remaining baking time.) Remove from the oven and let cool for 15 minutes.

5. Serve warm or at room temperature with vanilla ice cream, if you like.

HOW TO STORE
The best way to store leftover galette is to allow it to cool completely, then wrap tightly and refrigerate. Rewarm in a 350°F (175°C) oven for about 10 minutes, until warmed throughout. Galette, like pie, will get soggy starting on the third day.

LIGHT & LEMONY JELLY ROLL WITH RASPBERRY CREAM FILLING

DATE FLUCTUATES | Vernal Equinox
Yield **1 jelly roll cake • 12 to 16 pieces**

In New York, spring is an ideal. It is a reason to be. It is an awakening from the deep winter doldrums and liberation from bulky winter jackets. It's blue skies, low humidity, open windows, crayon-colored farmers' markets, and lightweight hoodies. The streets are infused with a renewed vigor; random smiles are infectious and everywhere. Unfortunately, spring is relatively short in New York. Summer, brutal and ugly and fragrant (not in a good way), is always nipping at the heels of our precious spring. Though spring may be brief, and though it is sandwiched between two less desirable seasons, it is welcome and celebratory and reason enough to move to New York City.

There are a million ways to celebrate spring via dessert, but we prefer the light and lemony route. We also happen to think a little retro flair—here, a jelly roll—is always in order. This dessert is extraordinarily light and bright with lemon flavor. The raspberry cream filling is a superb cake companion (and, by the by, incredibly addictive, so much so that we often "accidentally" eat—in the name of testing—quite a bit of frosting before it makes it to the cake). This cake is crowd-pleasing in that "wow, you rolled up a cake" kind of way. Do not fear the jelly roll—practice does indeed make perfect.

BAKED NOTE

When buying any extract (including lemon), use only brands marked pure and natural. If you have trouble locating pure and natural lemon extract, you can substitute a pure and natural lemon "flavor" (often the same size as most extract bottles and often more ubiquitous) for the extract in this recipe; just use ½ teaspoon instead.

MAKE THE LEMON CAKE

1. Preheat the oven to 400°F (205°C). Lightly coat the bottom and sides of a half sheet pan with nonstick cooking spray and line it with parchment paper. Lightly spray the parchment with the nonstick cooking spray.

continued on p. 180

LIGHT & LEMONY JELLY ROLL WITH RASPBERRY CREAM FILLING *continued*

FOR THE LEMON CAKE

1 cup (130 g) cake flour

1 teaspoon baking powder

5 large eggs, at room temperature, separated

1 cup (200 g) granulated sugar

Zest of 5 lemons (about 5 tablespoons)

1 teaspoon lemon extract (see Baked Note on p. 179)

¼ teaspoon cream of tartar

¼ teaspoon kosher salt

2 tablespoons confectioners' sugar

FOR THE RASPBERRY CREAM FILLING

1¾ cups (225 g) fresh raspberries

1¾ cups (420 ml) heavy cream

3 tablespoons confectioners' sugar

1 to 2 tablespoons Chambord liqueur (optional)

1 teaspoon pure vanilla extract

FOR THE ASSEMBLY

2 tablespoons confectioners' sugar, for dusting

Fresh raspberries, for garnish (optional)

2. Sift the flour and baking powder into a small bowl. Turn the sifted ingredients onto a piece of parchment paper and sift them together one more time into the bowl. Set aside.

3. Place the egg yolks in the bowl of a standing mixer fitted with the paddle attachment. Sprinkle ½ cup (100 g) granulated sugar over the yolks, and beat on high speed until the mixture ribbons and is very pale and thick, at least 5 minutes. Add the lemon zest and lemon extract. Beat until just combined, about 15 seconds. Transfer the mixture to a large bowl, and clean and dry the mixer bowl.

4. Place the egg whites in the clean bowl and fit the standing mixer with the whisk attachment; beat on medium-high speed for 1 minute. Sprinkle the cream of tartar and salt over the egg whites and continue beating on medium-high until soft peaks begin to form, 3 to 5 minutes. Reduce the speed to medium, then slowly stream in the remaining ½ cup (100 g) granulated sugar and continue beating until the whites are glossy and stiff but not dry.

5. Using a rubber spatula, gently fold one-third of the beaten egg whites into the yolk mixture. Gently fold half of the sifted flour mixture into the yolk mixture, then half of the remaining egg whites. Gently fold in the remaining flour mixture, followed by the remaining egg whites. Transfer the batter into the prepared pan and very gently smooth the top into an even layer with an offset spatula. Bake the cake until it begins to pull away from the sides, 5 to 8 minutes; keep a keen eye on it the whole time to avoid overbaking. You can also test for doneness by gently pressing in the center with your finger: If the cake springs back, it is done.

6. Transfer the pan to a cooling rack, cover the cake with a few damp (but not wet) paper towels, and cool for 10 minutes. Run a knife under hot water, wipe dry, then run the knife around the edges of the still-warm cake. Remove the paper towels and sift 1 tablespoon confectioners' sugar over the cake. Drape a very thin tea towel over the cake, then place a half sheet pan right side up on top of the tea towel. With a quick motion, invert the cake onto the back of the clean sheet pan, and remove the baking pan. Gently remove the parchment paper. Sift the remaining tablespoon of confectioners' sugar over the cake. Trim a scant ¼ inch (6 mm) off all sides of the cake. Starting with a short side of the cake, roll the cake up ever so gently, using the towel to support the cake as you go (it's almost like a lift and turn motion)—the towel itself will roll up in the cake. Let the cake cool all rolled up in the towel, seam side down.

continued on p. 182

LIGHT & LEMONY JELLY ROLL WITH RASPBERRY CREAM FILLING *continued*

MAKE THE RASPBERRY CREAM FILLING

1. Chill the bowl of the standing mixer.

2. Slice ¼ cup (roughly 1 ounce/28 g) of the raspberries in half and set aside.

3. Place the remaining raspberries in a food processor or blender and process or blend until completely pureed. Push the raspberry mixture through a fine-mesh sieve into a large bowl. Discard the seeds left behind.

4. Place the cream in the chilled mixer bowl and fit the mixer with the whisk attachment; whisk on medium speed for 1 minute. Sprinkle the confectioners' sugar over the cream, then continue to beat until soft peaks form, 3 to 5 minutes. Add the Chambord, if using, a tablespoon at a time, to taste, and the vanilla, and beat again until incorporated. Gently fold in the raspberry puree until the mixture is almost but not completely uniform (the striations in the mixture make it more visually interesting).

ASSEMBLE THE JELLY ROLL

1. Unroll the cake gently onto a sheet of parchment on a flat surface. Spread the raspberry filling over the cake in an even layer. Sprinkle the sliced raspberries over the cream. Gently roll the cake back up, as tightly as possible (use the towel to help guide the cake if needed, but do not roll the towel into the cake). Place the cake, seam side down, on a serving plate, sift confectioners' sugar over the top, cover gently with plastic wrap, and refrigerate for 1 hour to set.

2. To serve, garnish with more raspberries, if you like, slice, and serve immediately.

HOW TO STORE

The cake can be stored, tightly covered, in the refrigerator for 2 days (though it tastes best within 24 hours); allow it to sit out at room temperature for about 30 minutes before serving.

FUDGY RASPBERRY SWIRL BROWNIES

Active **25 min**; Total **1 hr plus cooling and chilling**; Makes **24 brownies**

Matt Lewis and Renato Poliafito revere the brownie: "It is an American dessert institution—and we treat it with a lot of care and respect." The fudgy, chewy ones here are laced with a bright, tangy puree of fresh raspberries; they're especially good lightly chilled.

- 1½ sticks unsalted butter, cut into 1-inch pieces, plus more for greasing
- 1 cup fresh raspberries
- 1¼ cups all-purpose flour
- 2 tablespoons unsweetened cocoa powder
- 1 teaspoon kosher salt
- 11 ounces dark chocolate (60 to 72 percent), coarsely chopped
- 1 cup granulated sugar
- ½ cup packed light brown sugar
- 5 large eggs, at room temperature
- 1½ teaspoons pure vanilla extract

1. Preheat the oven to 350°F. Butter a 9-inch square baking pan. In a food processor, puree the raspberries. Strain the puree through a fine sieve to remove the seeds, if desired.

2. In a medium bowl, whisk the flour, cocoa powder and salt. In a large heatproof bowl set over a pan of barely simmering water, combine the 1½ sticks of butter and the chocolate. Cook over moderate heat, stirring occasionally, until the chocolate and butter are completely melted and blended, about 4 minutes. Remove from the heat and whisk in the granulated sugar and brown sugar, then whisk in 3 of the eggs. Add the remaining 2 eggs and whisk until just combined. Stir in the vanilla. Using a rubber spatula, fold in the flour mixture until it is barely visible.

3. Scrape the batter into the prepared baking pan and smooth the top. Drizzle the raspberry puree over the batter and swirl it in with a table knife. Bake the brownies, rotating the pan once, until a tester inserted in the center comes out with a few moist crumbs attached, about 40 minutes. Let cool completely on a rack, then refrigerate until cool, about 20 minutes. Serve lightly chilled.

FOR MORE ON MATT LEWIS & RENATO POLIAFITO

bakednyc.com
BAKED
@brooklynbaker

HUNGRY FOR FRANCE

Adventures for the Cook & Food Lover

BY ALEXANDER LOBRANO WITH RECIPES BY JANE SIGAL

When writer Alexander Lobrano relocated to Paris 30 years ago, he had an epiphany: "I'd been so excited by the idea of moving to Paris that I overlooked the fact that I was getting France in the bargain." The excursions that followed inspired this book, with stellar recipes by former *Food & Wine* editor Jane Sigal. As a lonely expat, Lobrano met some friendly locals in Alsace, who tutored him on classic dishes—the impetus for a recipe of spaetzle with chorizo crumbs (p. 190). He also focuses on current trends, sharing a recipe for spinach pasta with buttery pistou (p. 187) from a bistro run by a former Michelin-starred chef. Lobrano defies the haters who've been "kicking France's ankles in a double-decade-long takedown of Gallic gastronomic superiority." With this book, he makes a strong case for France's enduring greatness.

Published by Rizzoli, $45

TOMATO-RUBBED TOASTS WITH MARINATED HAM

Makes **4 entrée servings**

¼ cup (60 ml) extra-virgin olive oil

1½ Tbsp. red wine vinegar

2 pickled jalapeños, thinly sliced

2 shallots, thinly sliced

Kosher salt and piment d'Espelette

4 very thin slices Serrano ham

4 slices sourdough bread, cut ½ inch (1 cm) thick

2 ripe tomatoes, cut in half horizontally

Fleur de sel

Snipped chives or chopped scallions, for sprinkling

EDITOR'S WINE CHOICE
Lively, dry Provençal rosé.

In Ahetze, La Ferme Ostalapia's by-the-book pain tomate *is served with Serrano ham and the local pickled peppers, guindillas. In this variation, the tomato toasts are topped with grilled ham slices spiked with shallot-chile vinaigrette.*

1. In a large gratin dish, whisk oil with vinegar, jalapeños, shallots, kosher salt, and piment d'Espelette until smooth.
DO AHEAD *Vinaigrette can be refrigerated overnight.*

2. Heat a grill or a grill pan until hot. Grill ham slices over medium-high heat just until edges begin to brown, a few seconds per side. Transfer ham to vinaigrette and turn to coat.

3. Grill bread slices until crisp and nicely browned, 2 to 4 minutes per side; transfer to a platter or plates. Rub bread slices with cut tomatoes and top with ham and vinaigrette. Season with fleur de sel, sprinkle with chives, and serve.

SPINACH FETTUCCINE WITH BUTTERY PISTOU

Makes **6 appetizer or 4 entrée servings**

Kosher salt

1 lb. (500 g) fresh spinach fettuccine

2 cups (60 g) packed basil

¼ cup (60 ml) extra-virgin olive oil

2 garlic cloves, sliced

Fleur de sel

¼ cup (30 g) freshly grated Parmesan cheese

¼ cup (30 g) freshly grated Emmenthal cheese

2 Tbsp. (30 g) unsalted butter, diced

Freshly ground pepper

EDITOR'S WINE CHOICE
Fragrant, full-bodied Rhône white.

At his humble bistro, La Merenda, in Nice, Dominique Le Stanc, who once earned two Michelin stars at the luxe Hôtel Negresco nearby, gives his pâtes au pistou *the attention of a multistar meal. He picks green pasta instead of white, forgoes the usual pine nuts in his* pistou (the local pesto), *and finishes the dish with Emmenthal cheese and butter for subtle richness.*

1. In a large saucepan of boiling salted water, cook fettuccine, stirring occasionally, until tender; drain.

2. Meanwhile, in a food processor, puree basil with oil, garlic, and fleur de sel until smooth. Transfer pistou to a large shallow bowl. Add Parmesan, Emmenthal, and butter. Add fettuccine, season with fleur de sel and pepper, and toss until butter and cheese melt creamily. Serve immediately.

GRATINÉED CHICKEN WITH MIMOLETTE CHEESE

Makes **4 entrée servings**

¼ cup (60 ml) grapeseed oil

1½ lb. (750 g) white mushrooms, sliced

Kosher salt and freshly ground pepper

2 Tbsp. (30 g) unsalted butter

2 Tbsp. (20 g) all-purpose flour

2 cups (500 ml) chicken stock

1 cup (250 ml) crème fraîche or sour cream

One 3½-lb. (1.5-kg) chicken, cut into 8 pieces

6 thyme sprigs

3 oz. (90 g) aged Mimolette, Edam, or Gouda cheese, freshly grated

EDITOR'S WINE CHOICE
Fruit-forward, minerally white, such as Pinot Gris from Alsace.

In French Flanders, cheese makers produce a nutty orange Mimolette with a distinctive pockmarked rind. The flavorful aged variety is an especially good grating cheese for this rich gratin from L'Estaminet de l'Ancienne Maison in Hondeghem. Serve with steamed rice or quinoa for soaking up the creamy sauce.

1. Heat oven to 475°F (245°C). In a large skillet, heat 2 tablespoons oil until very hot. Add mushrooms and season with salt and pepper. Cook over medium-high heat, stirring occasionally, until water released has evaporated, about 7 minutes. Spread in a medium gratin dish.

2. In a medium saucepan, melt butter. Add flour and cook over low heat, whisking, for 3 minutes. Add stock, bring to a simmer, and cook over medium-high heat, whisking occasionally, until reduced by half, 10 to 15 minutes. Remove pan from heat and whisk in crème fraîche. Season with salt and pepper.

DO AHEAD *Mushrooms and cream sauce can be refrigerated for up to 4 hours; heat oven when ready to bake.*

3. Set a large cast-iron or other heavy ovenproof skillet over high heat until very hot. Season chicken pieces with salt and pepper. Reduce heat to medium-high and add remaining 2 tablespoons oil. Add chicken, skin side down, and thyme and cook until skin is browned, about 5 minutes.

4. Turn chicken skin side up and transfer skillet to oven floor or lowest rack. Roast chicken until breast juices run clear, about 10 minutes. Transfer breasts to gratin dish. Return skillet to oven and cook until leg juices run clear, another 5 to 10 minutes. Transfer legs to gratin dish. Discard thyme.

5. Pour cream sauce over chicken and sprinkle with cheese. Transfer dish to oven and bake, rotating dish halfway through, until cheese has melted and is lightly browned, about 15 minutes. Serve directly from gratin dish.

SPAETZLE WITH SPICY CRUMBS

Makes **4 side servings**

1 cup (130 g) all-purpose flour

Kosher salt and freshly ground pepper

2 large eggs

½ cup (125 ml) milk

1 oz. (30 g) Spanish chorizo or other spicy, dry salami, sliced

½ cup (25 g) panko

4 Tbsp. (60 g) unsalted butter

The clever idea here is pulsing chorizo with bread crumbs to add a ton of extra flavor and great crunch to Alsace's gnocchi-like dumplings, spaetzle. Serve with roasted or braised beef, pork, or chicken.

1. In a medium bowl, whisk flour with ½ teaspoon salt and ⅛ teaspoon pepper and make a well in center. Add eggs to well and lightly beat them. Stir flour into eggs. Gradually stir in milk until a thick batter forms. Cover bowl with plastic wrap and let stand for 30 minutes.

2. Meanwhile, in a mini food processor, pulse chorizo until finely chopped. Add panko and pulse just to combine.

3. In a large nonstick skillet, melt 2 tablespoons (30 grams) butter over medium heat. Add crumb mixture and cook, stirring, until crisp and golden, about 2 minutes. Transfer crumbs to a plate and wipe out skillet.

4. Bring a large saucepan of salted water to a boil. Using a flexible spatula, scrape batter into a colander with ¼-inch (6-mm) holes set or held 1 inch (2.5 cm) above water. Press batter through holes. Cook spaetzle, stirring occasionally, until they rise to surface, about 2 minutes. Drain spaetzle in a colander.
DO AHEAD *Spaetzle can be refrigerated overnight.*

5. In same nonstick skillet, melt remaining 2 tablespoons (30 grams) butter. Add spaetzle and cook over medium-high heat, stirring occasionally, until lightly browned, about 5 minutes. Season with salt and pepper. Transfer spaetzle to a shallow bowl, sprinkle with crumbs, and serve.

WATERCRESS SOUP WITH MUSSELS

Total **1 hr**; Serves **4**

- 2 tablespoons unsalted butter
- 1 large shallot, finely chopped
- 1 celery rib, finely chopped
- 1 thyme sprig
- 1 bay leaf
- Salt
- 1 pound small mussels, scrubbed and debearded
- 1 cup dry white wine
- 1 small Yukon Gold potato, peeled and finely diced
- 1 large bunch of watercress (6 ounces), thick stems discarded, the rest coarsely chopped
- ¼ cup heavy cream
- Pepper

"In Normandy, mussels are often prepared à la marinière— steamed with white wine, shallot and herbs," according to Jane Sigal. Here, she cleverly uses the cooking liquid as the base for a light, peppery watercress soup, which she garnishes with shucked mussels.

1. In a medium saucepan, melt the butter. Add the shallot, celery, thyme, bay leaf and a pinch of salt and cook over moderate heat, stirring, until softened, 5 minutes. Stir in the mussels and wine, cover and cook, shaking the pan occasionally, until the mussels open, 4 to 5 minutes. Using a slotted spoon, transfer the mussels to a bowl. Discard any that do not open. Remove the mussels from their shells and keep them warm.

2. Carefully pour the cooking liquid, vegetables and herbs into a large saucepan, leaving the grit behind. Add the potato and 2 cups of water and bring to a boil over high heat. Stir in the watercress, cover and cook over moderate heat, stirring occasionally, until the potato is tender, about 15 minutes.

3. Discard the thyme sprig and bay leaf. Working in batches if necessary, puree the soup in a blender until smooth. Return the soup to the saucepan, stir in the cream and bring to a simmer. Season with salt and pepper. Ladle the soup into shallow bowls, garnish with the mussels and serve.

FOR MORE ON ALEXANDER LOBRANO & JANE SIGAL
alexanderlobrano.com, janesigal.com
🐦 @AlecLobrano, @JaneSigal

Oat flour

FLAVOR FLOURS

A New Way to Bake with Teff, Buckwheat, Sorghum, Other Whole & Ancient Grains, Nuts & Non-Wheat Flours

BY ALICE MEDRICH WITH MAYA KLEIN

Alice Medrich began experimenting with flours made from buckwheat, coconut and chestnuts after growing curious about the ingredients she'd been ignoring in the baking aisle. "I'd been just walking by them for so long, when I finally stopped one day and said to myself, 'I'm a pastry chef. These are ingredients. Why am I not paying attention to them?'" Here, the master baker shares recipes for 12 flours that showcase the unique flavor affinities and baking personalities of each. Buckwheat flour gives her cinnamon-scented pumpkin loaf (p. 198) a slightly woodsy flavor; brown rice flour adds a wonderful caramel flavor to a tres leches cake (p. 200). Treating each flour as a "hero" ingredient rather than a gluten-free compromise, Medrich introduces us to a new world of flavor. "If you discovered a new fruit that you weren't used to eating," she asks, "wouldn't you want to taste it?"

Published by Artisan, $35

WALNUT & BUCKWHEAT CRACKERS

Makes **1½ dozen large crackers**

1 cup plus 2 tablespoons (100 grams) brown rice flour

¾ cup (120 grams) white rice flour *or* 1¼ cups (120 grams) Thai white rice flour

½ cup (60 grams) buckwheat flour

1 cup (100 grams) walnut pieces

¼ cup plus 2 tablespoons (40 grams) flaxseed meal or ¼ cup (40 grams) whole flaxseed, finely ground

1 tablespoon brown sugar

1½ teaspoons salt

¾ cup plus 1 tablespoon water

1 tablespoon rice vinegar

2 teaspoons baking powder

¼ cup flavorless vegetable oil (such as soybean, corn, or safflower)

EQUIPMENT

Stand mixer with paddle attachment

Rolling pin

Baking sheets

Dark and crunchy and pleasingly bitter, these crackers are fabulous with a smear of whole-milk Greek yogurt or sour cream topped with lox or salmon roe (or real caviar) and very thinly sliced red onions or shallots. These crackers keep well and are fantastic to package in cellophane bags and give as a hostess gift. The recipe can be doubled or tripled with ease.

Position racks in the upper and lower thirds of the oven and preheat the oven to 450°F.

Mix the flours, walnuts, flaxseed meal, brown sugar, and salt in the bowl of the stand mixer fitted with the paddle attachment. Add the water and vinegar and beat for 2 minutes on medium speed to form a very thick, sticky dough that might wrap around the paddle at first. Sprinkle in the baking powder, add the oil, and beat for 1 minute on medium speed to thoroughly incorporate the oil.

Cut four pieces of parchment the size of a baking sheet. Drop three 2-tablespoon lumps of dough evenly spaced down the length of a parchment sheet. Cover with another piece of parchment and flatten each lump with the heel of your hand. Use a rolling pin to roll the dough into oblongs about 3 by 5 inches to about 4 by 8 inches (for even thinner crackers) and a scant ⅛ inch thick. Peel off the top parchment (save for reuse) and place the parchment with the crackers *dough side down* on a baking sheet.

Bake for 5 to 6 minutes, two pans at a time, rotating them from upper to lower and front to back for even baking, until the crackers are browned at the edges. Remove the pan from the oven and carefully peel off the parchment (save for reuse). Flip the crackers over with a spatula and return them to the oven for 2 to 3 minutes, or until well browned at the edges. Repeat with the remaining dough: while the crackers are baking, continue to roll out more dough; as soon as the pans of crackers are done, flip the next batch onto the baking sheets (it's okay if the sheets are still hot as long as you put them in the oven immediately).

Cool the crackers thoroughly on parchment or a rack before storing in an airtight container for up to 10 days. Crackers may be refreshed before serving by baking for 5 minutes at 400°F.

WALNUT ALFAJORES

Makes **twenty 2-inch cookies**

Scant ½ cup (50 grams)
coconut flour

1½ cups (150 grams) walnut
pieces

¼ teaspoon baking powder

½ teaspoon salt

1 cup plus 2 tablespoons
(225 grams) sugar

6 tablespoons (85 grams)
unsalted butter, very soft

1 teaspoon pure vanilla extract

1 large egg white

⅔ cup dulce de leche or cajeta

EQUIPMENT

Food processor fitted with
the steel blade

2 baking sheets, lined with
parchment paper

Alfajores are luscious sandwich cookies filled with dulce de leche or cajeta (goat's-milk caramel available in cans or squeeze bottles from better supermarkets and Hispanic groceries). Every region makes alfajores with a different type of cookie, so I never hesitate to invent my own new combinations. Here, the sweet caramelized milk balances the bitter tannins in the walnuts perfectly. If you're a fan of Nutella, you can use it to fill the cookies instead of the dulce de leche.

Combine the coconut flour, walnuts, baking powder, salt, and sugar in the bowl of the food processor. Process until the walnuts are finely ground, about 15 seconds. Add the butter, vanilla, and egg white and pulse 8 to 10 times, or until the dough comes together. Form the mixture into a 10-inch log on a sheet of wax or parchment paper. Wrap the log in the paper, keeping it as cylindrical as possible. Chill for at least 2 hours and up to 3 days, or wrap airtight and freeze for up to 3 months. Thaw before using.

Position the oven racks in the upper and lower thirds of the oven and preheat the oven to 350°F.

Use a thin serrated knife to cut the dough into slices a scant ¼ inch thick. Place the slices 1 inch apart on the lined sheets. Bake for 9 to 11 minutes, until the cookies are golden on the bottom and browned at the edges; rotate the baking sheets from top to bottom and front to back halfway through the baking time. Set the pans on racks to cool completely or slide the parchment liners onto racks to cool. Repeat with the remaining dough.

When the cookies are completely cooled, fill with dulce de leche. Turn half of the cookies upside down. Spoon dulce de leche into one corner of a resealable plastic freezer bag. Clip about ¼ inch from the corner and pipe about 1½ teaspoons onto each upside-down cookie. Cover with a right-side-up cookie and press very gently to spread the filling toward the edges.

The cookies will keep in an airtight container for up to 3 days, although they will soften after the first day. Unfilled cookies may be stored for up to 1 week.

DARK & SPICY PUMPKIN LOAF

Serves **6 to 8**

8 tablespoons (1 stick/ 115 grams) unsalted butter, melted

1 cup (200 grams) sugar

2 large eggs

¾ cup (120 grams) white rice flour *or* 1¼ cups (120 grams) Thai white rice flour

⅓ cup (40 grams) buckwheat flour

½ teaspoon baking soda

1 teaspoon baking powder

1 teaspoon ground cinnamon

½ teaspoon ground nutmeg

¼ teaspoon salt

¾ cup (170 grams) pumpkin puree

½ cup (70 grams) raisins or currants

EQUIPMENT

8½-by-4½-inch (6-cup) loaf pan, bottom and all four sides lined with parchment paper

Stand mixer with paddle attachment or handheld mixer

Buckwheat flour lends an almost woodsy note to the flavor of this not-too-sweet tea cake. Serve it with coffee, plain or with a smear of cream cheese or soft goat cheese. The batter may also be baked in muffin cups or it may be doubled and baked in a Bundt pan.

Position a rack in the lower third of the oven and preheat the oven to 350°F. Line the bottom and sides of the loaf pan with parchment paper.

Combine the butter, sugar, and eggs in the bowl of the stand mixer and beat on medium speed with the paddle attachment until lighter in color, about 2 minutes. Or beat with the handheld mixer in a large bowl on medium-high speed for 3 to 4 minutes.

Add the rice and buckwheat flours, baking soda, baking powder, cinnamon, nutmeg, salt, pumpkin puree, and raisins and beat on low speed until smooth. Scrape the mixture into the prepared pan.

Bake the loaf for 45 to 50 minutes, until a toothpick inserted in the center comes out clean. Cool the loaf in the pan on a rack for at least 2 hours before unmolding and slicing.

The cake keeps, wrapped airtight, in the refrigerator for up to 5 days; let come to room temperature to serve.

BROWN RICE SPONGE CAKE WITH THREE MILKS

Serves **10 to 12**

FOR THE CAKE

- **6 tablespoons (85 grams) clarified butter or ghee**
- **¾ cup (100 grams) brown rice flour, preferably superfine**
- **⅔ cup (130 grams) sugar**
- **4 large eggs**
- **⅛ teaspoon salt**

FOR THE SAUCE

- **1 can (12 ounces) evaporated milk**
- **1 generous cup (350 grams) purchased dulce de leche or cajeta**
- **⅛ teaspoon salt**

- **Whipped cream, unsweetened or very lightly sweetened**

EQUIPMENT

- **8-by-2-inch round cake pan**
- **Stand mixer with whisk attachment**
- **Sifter or medium-mesh strainer**

Of course you could serve this buttery sponge cake plain (or splashed with a little sweetened espresso or coffee liqueur) and topped with strawberries and whipped cream. But the brown rice flour adds a delicate caramel flavor to the cake, so why not run with it? This riff on the traditional Latin American tres leches—sponge cake drenched in a combo of heavy cream, sweetened condensed milk, and evaporated milk—is less sweet and less drenched than the authentic version, but a terrific variation nonetheless. The warm or cooled cake is poked with a chopstick or the not-too-thick handle of a wooden spoon and then soaked with a sauce of dulce de leche and evaporated milk. The third "milk" is whipped cream on top. More sauce is passed separately at table. What could be more delicious?

Position a rack in the lower third of the oven and preheat the oven to 350°F. Line the bottom of the pan with parchment paper, but do not grease the sides of the pan.

Put the clarified butter in a small pot or microwavable container ready to reheat when needed, and have a 4- to 5-cup bowl ready to pour it into as well—the bowl must be big enough to allow you to fold some batter into the butter later.

Whisk the flour and 2 tablespoons of the sugar together thoroughly in a medium bowl.

Combine the remaining sugar, eggs, and salt in the bowl of the stand mixer and beat with the whisk attachment on high speed for at least 5 minutes. The mixture should be light colored and tripled in volume, and you should see well-defined tracks as the whisk spins; when the whisk is lifted, the mixture should fall in a thick, fluffy rope that dissolves slowly on the surface of the batter.

Just before the eggs are ready, heat the clarified butter until very hot and pour it into the reserved bowl.

continued on p. 202

BROWN RICE SPONGE CAKE
WITH THREE MILKS *continued*

Remove the bowl from the mixer. Sift one-third of the flour over the eggs. Fold with a large rubber spatula until the flour is almost blended into the batter. Repeat with half of the remaining flour. Repeat with the rest of the flour. Scrape about a quarter of the batter into the hot butter. Fold until the butter is completely blended into the batter. Scrape the buttery batter over the remaining batter and fold just until blended. Scrape the batter into the pan.

Bake for 30 to 35 minutes, until the cake is golden brown on top. It will have puffed up and then settled level, but it won't have pulled away from the sides of the pan and a toothpick inserted in the center will come out clean and dry. Set the pan on a rack. While the cake is still hot, run a small spatula around the inside of the pan, pressing against the sides of the pan to avoid tearing the cake.

At your convenience (the cake can be warm or completely cool), invert the pan to remove the cake and peel off the parchment liner. Turn the cake right side up. (The cake should be completely cool before storing.) The cake may be wrapped airtight and stored at room temperature for 2 days, or frozen for up to 3 months.

To assemble the cake, an hour (or up to several hours) before serving, set the cake (cooled or warm) on a rimmed serving platter and poke holes 1 inch apart all over it with a chopstick or a thin wooden spoon handle. Make the sauce by stirring the evaporated milk, dulce de leche, and salt together until smooth. Spoon 1½ to 2 cups of the sauce over the cake, a little at a time, allowing it to be absorbed. Use the greater quantity if you want a more soaked cake, or let some of the delicious cake remain dry. Either way, pass the extra sauce at the table. Make sure the cake is completely cool before topping it with swirls of unsweetened or very lightly sweetened whipped cream, leaving the sides bare. Refrigerate the cake in a covered container or under a cake dome. Leftover cake keeps in the refrigerator for a few days.

BLUEBERRY TART WITH AN OAT FLOUR CRUST

Active **30 min**; Total **5 hr (includes cooling and chilling)**; Makes **one 9-inch tart**

CRUST

- 6 tablespoons unsalted butter, softened, plus more for greasing the pan
- ¾ cup oat flour
- 3 tablespoons white rice flour
- ¼ cup sugar
- ⅛ teaspoon salt
- 1/16 teaspoon baking soda
- 2 tablespoons cream cheese, softened
- ½ teaspoon pure vanilla extract

FILLING

- 3 cups blueberries
- ¾ cup sugar
- 1 tablespoon cornstarch
- 1 teaspoon finely grated lemon zest
- ⅛ teaspoon salt

"The combination of raw and cooked berries is irresistible," says Alice Medrich about this outstanding tart. She has a secret for creating an even crust that bakes up crisp and tender: Press a sheet of plastic wrap against the bottom and up the sides of the dough, then place a paper towel on top. Use the bottom of a straight-sided, flat-bottom measuring cup to smooth the surface.

1. Make the crust Butter a 9-inch fluted tart pan with a removable bottom. In a large bowl, whisk together the oat flour, rice flour, sugar, salt and baking soda. Add the 6 tablespoons of butter, the cream cheese and the vanilla; mash and mix with a fork or the back of a large spoon until a smooth, soft dough forms.

2. Press the dough into the tart pan using your fingers or a small offset spatula: Spread the dough evenly all over the bottom of the pan and up the sides. Press a sheet of plastic wrap onto the dough and refrigerate for at least 2 hours and up to 3 days.

3. Preheat the oven to 325°F. Set the pan on a baking sheet and bake in the lower third of the oven, rotating once, until the crust is golden brown and has pulled away from the sides of the pan, 30 to 35 minutes. If the crust puffs up too much after 15 to 20 minutes of baking, press it down gently with the back of a fork. The crust can be filled immediately or cooled completely.

4. Make the filling Spread 1 cup of the blueberries in the baked crust. In a medium saucepan, combine the remaining 2 cups of blueberries with the sugar, cornstarch, lemon zest, salt and ⅓ cup of water. Bring to a simmer over moderate heat, stirring frequently, about 10 minutes; continue to cook, stirring frequently, until the filling is thick and translucent, about 2 minutes longer. Scrape the blueberry mixture over the raw blueberries in the crust and spread in an even layer. Let cool, then refrigerate for at least 1 hour, or until the filling is set.

5. Unmold the tart and transfer to a platter. Serve chilled.

FOR MORE ON ALICE MEDRICH
alicemedrich.com
Alice Medrich
@AliceMedrich

The club members gather each week to debate which recipes to include in their books. All profits from their books' sales go to charity.

THE FEAST GOES ON

BY THE MONDAY MORNING COOKING CLUB: LISA GOLDBERG, MERELYN FRANK CHALMERS, NATANYA ESKIN, LAUREN FINK, PAULA HORWITZ & JACQUI ISRAEL

The six women of this Sydney-based club have a calling: to rescue traditional Jewish cooking, one recipe at a time. For founding member Lisa Goldberg, the catalyst was the death of her aunt Myrna, a platinum blonde from Poland who made phenomenal cabbage rolls (p. 212). "Our mission is to find all the Aunty Myrnas in the world and save their recipes before it's too late," says Goldberg. For *The Feast Goes On*, the club asked Jewish home cooks from all over Australia to send in heirloom family recipes. The results show the remarkable culinary legacy of the Jewish diaspora, as in a dish of snapper fillets with buttery wheat bulgur pilaf (p. 210) passed down to a Turkish émigré, who cooks it to remind his children of their cultural heritage.

Published by HarperCollins, $35

SPINACH & FETA COILS
—JACK SAGES

Serves **8 to 10**

8 to 10 sheets filo pastry

1 bunch English spinach, about 6½ oz (180 g) leaves

9 oz (250 g) feta cheese

3½ oz (100 g) pecorino cheese, grated

3½ oz (100 g) parmesan cheese, grated

1 tablespoon plain (all-purpose) flour

2 eggs

3½ oz (100 g) butter, melted

Scant ½ cup (100 ml) vegetable oil

1 egg, lightly beaten, for glazing

Sesame seeds

EDITOR'S WINE CHOICE
Zippy, fresh northern Italian Pinot Grigio.

These are a wonderful and impressive pastry to serve as a light meal, but are so simple to make. Serve hot alongside a simple green salad for lunch. It's best to take the filo out of the fridge at least 2 hours before making to allow the coils to be rolled more easily.

Take the filo pastry out of the fridge at least 2 hours before starting the recipe to minimise cracking when shaping the coils.

Preheat the oven to 400°F (200°C/Gas 6). Line two baking trays.

Wash the spinach, remove and discard the large stems and chop the leaves. Blanch in boiling water, then drain thoroughly. Leave to cool slightly, then squeeze out as much excess water as possible. The cooked spinach should weigh about 3 oz (85 g).

Crumble the feta into a bowl, add the other cheeses, flour, eggs and spinach and mix well.

Combine the melted butter and oil in a bowl.

Place 1 sheet of the filo in front of you vertically on the benchtop. Cover the remaining sheets with a damp cloth. Lightly brush the butter mixture over the filo sheet, ensuring the entire surface is covered. Make a 1½ inch (4 cm) fold at the short end of the pastry sheet, then spread a ¾ inch (2 cm) thick layer of the spinach filling over this fold from left to right, leaving about ¾ inch (2 cm) space at both ends.

Fold both the long sides of the pastry inwards to prevent leakage, then roll the pastry up from the bottom to the top to make a cylinder. Wrap the cylinder into a coil shape and place on a prepared tray. Repeat the process with the remaining filling and filo sheets until you have 8 to 10 coils. Brush the tops with beaten egg and sprinkle over the sesame seeds. Bake for 25 to 30 minutes until golden brown. Use a paper towel to remove any excess oil before serving.

SHAVED FENNEL & MINT SALAD

–LISA LIPSHUT

Serves **8**

1 fennel bulb, about 1 lb (450 g), fronds reserved

6 to 8 (160 g) small radishes

6 to 8 (180 g) brussels sprouts

1½ cups (240 g) peas, blanched

1 long red chilli, deseeded and finely sliced

1 large handful mint leaves, torn

1 heaped cup (100 g) walnuts

5½ oz (150 g) goat's cheese, crumbled

DRESSING

5 tablespoons (100 ml) lemon juice

2 tablespoons sherry vinegar

Scant ½ cup (100 ml) olive oil

¾ teaspoon sea salt

Freshly ground black pepper

When making salads I have learned to adjust ingredients according to visual balance and personal likings. If a salad calls for feta cheese but someone loves goat's cheese, then I use that instead. I like to use a large, lightweight mixing bowl to toss the salad and then transfer it to the serving dish, adjusting for colour and appearance if needed.

Use a mandoline or sharp knife to very finely slice the fennel, radishes and brussels sprouts. Place in a bowl and add the peas, fennel fronds, chilli and mint. Toss together gently.

To make the dressing, in a small bowl, whisk together the lemon juice, sherry vinegar, olive oil, salt and pepper.

Toss the salad with the dressing, then garnish with the walnuts and goat's cheese.

I fell in love with food because of my late dad. He never ceased to amaze us with his wild culinary concoctions. I still remember waking up on a Sunday morning to the smells of his cooking wafting through the house. Dad cooked because he loved seeing others enjoying his food. I am the same, always encouraging people to try new things and simply being happy in the kitchen, cooking for my family of boys.

On weekends away with my lifelong girlfriends, it has become a tradition that I plan our menus—I put my "sous chefs" to work with strict orders (they are usually pretty obedient!) and over a glass of wine we cook, laugh and cry together, and then sit down to enjoy the fruits of our labour. The next day we do it all again. I remember reading somewhere that your mood is captured in your cooking so I do believe my family and friends can taste the love I put into my food.

CLAY POT SNAPPER WITH BURGHUL PILAF
—ATA GOKYILDIRIM

Serves **4**

1 lb 10 oz (750 g/about 4 large) snapper fillets, skin off

1½ tablespoons Ata's spice mix: equal quantities ground turmeric, sweet paprika, hot paprika, cumin, baharat, chilli (optional)

½ bunch flat-leaf (Italian) parsley, leaves only roughly chopped

1¾ oz (50 g) butter, chopped

Sea salt

1 lemon, sliced

1 tablespoon olive oil

Chopped fresh chilli or pickled peppers, for serving

BURGHUL PILAF

1 oz (30 g) butter

¼ cup (40 g) Turkish soup noodles or crushed fine vermicelli

1 heaped cup (200 g) medium coarse burghul (bulgur)

1½ cups (375 ml) boiling water

1 small handful flat-leaf (Italian) parsley leaves, roughly chopped

EDITOR'S WINE CHOICE
Ripe, fruity, medium-bodied California Sauvignon Blanc.

A simple dish of fresh fish with spices and a knob of butter served on top of nutty burghul. This is traditionally called "Adana" snapper and is made in a clay pot.

You will need a clay pot or a wide flat ovenproof dish.

Toss the fish with the spice mix, three-quarters of the parsley leaves and the butter and place in the clay pot or dish. Leave to marinate at room temperature for 30 minutes.

Preheat the oven to 410°F (210°C/Gas 6–7).

Season the fish generously with salt, top with the lemon slices and drizzle with the olive oil. Cover with foil or a lid and roast for 20 minutes. Remove the cover and return to the oven for 5 minutes, or until the fish is just cooked through.

Meanwhile, to make the burghul pilaf, melt the butter in a frying pan over medium heat. Add the noodles and toss, then add the burghul and cook in the butter for a minute. Add 1 cup of the water and stir. Cover with a lid, turn the heat down and cook for 5 minutes until the burghul softens and the water is absorbed. Add the remaining water, stir, cover with the lid and cook for a few minutes until the water is absorbed. If the burghul is not cooked once all the water has been absorbed, add a little more water and steam until just cooked. Add the parsley and season with salt.

Garnish the fish with the remaining parsley and serve with the burghul pilaf and the chilli on the side.

AUNTY MYRNA'S CABBAGE ROLLS

–MYRNA ABADEE

Serves **8**

1 green cabbage

SAUCE

2 onions, chopped

¼ cup (60 ml) vegetable oil

One 14¾ oz (420 g) tin condensed tomato soup

1½ cups (400 ml) tomato passata (puréed tomatoes)

One 14 oz (400 g) tin diced Italian tomatoes

Juice of 2 lemons

1½ tablespoons sugar

1 teaspoon salt

½ teaspoon freshly ground black pepper

FILLING

1 lb 5 oz (600 g) minced (ground) topside beef

2 to 3 cloves garlic

2 teaspoons sea salt

1 cup (185 g) cooked long-grain rice, about ½ cup (100 g) uncooked

1 onion, grated

½ teaspoon freshly ground black pepper

2 eggs, lightly beaten

EDITOR'S WINE CHOICE
Lively, red-berried Italian red, such as Barbera.

This is a dish that my aunty, Myrna Abadee, used to make often, as she would always have it ready in the fridge when friends dropped in for a bite. It is home cooking at its most heartwarming. I imagine the addition of tomato soup was introduced in Australia, when she tried to replicate the flavours of her own childhood. The flavours do improve if allowed to sit in the fridge for a couple of days. –Lisa Goldberg

Start this recipe at least one day before serving, as the flavours develop overnight.

Core the cabbage and place in a large saucepan of cold water so that the cabbage is fully submerged. Bring to the boil and simmer for 15 minutes. Remove from the stovetop and allow to cool in the water. Strain when cool, separate the leaves and cut out the thick stalks with a knife.

To make the sauce, you will need a large saucepan. Fry the onion in the oil over low heat until soft, about 20 minutes. Add the remaining ingredients and simmer for 15 minutes. Taste for seasoning. Set aside until needed.

To make the filling, put the beef in a medium-sized bowl. On a chopping board, using the back of a knife, press the garlic with the salt to form a paste. Add to the beef, along with the rice, onion and pepper. Season generously. Add the eggs and combine.

To make the parcels, lay ¼ cup of the filling in an oblong shape in the centre of a cabbage leaf. Fold in the ends and then roll up like a parcel. Place in the sauce, seam side down. Continue with all the filling and cabbage leaves, placing the rolls snugly side by side in the sauce. Any unused or torn leaves can be rolled up and stuffed into the gaps in the pan. Make sure all the rolls are covered with sauce. Bring to a simmer, cover and cook for 3 hours, basting from time to time. If the cabbage rolls start to dry out, add more water to cover.

Place in the refrigerator when cool and reheat to serve the next day.

LISA GOLDBERG:
I am the first to admit I am a fresser: dreaming, shopping, cooking, sharing, searching, ogling and photographing food and, of course, eating. I started professional life as a solicitor; since 2006 I have expressed this

continued on p. 214

AUNTY MYRNA'S CABBAGE ROLLS *continued*

passion for food, cooking and preserving recipes in heading the Monday Morning Cooking Club project. This project has changed my life and taken my obsession with food to a whole new level. I equally love standing at my stove trying something new as much as making my old favourites that no longer need a recipe.

My food inspiration stems a little from my mum, Paula, a little more from my bubba, Shendel, and my mother-in-law, Talia, but mostly from my Aunty Myrna. My father's older sister, who passed away in 2004, was a horserace-loving, cigarette-smoking, platinum blonde with a heart bigger than any. Polish-born, she immigrated to Melbourne as a young child in the 1930s with my father and their family. She had a wonderful broad Australian Carlton accent with just a hint of Eastern Europe. After Myrna married, she and her husband, Sol, ran a tiny shop—part newsagent and part delicatessen—where truck drivers and locals lined up for her superb homemade European delicacies.

Sitting at her vinyl-clothed kitchen table with the "wireless" on and the form guide open, she would force-feed me rugelach, tiny sultana strudels, butter chiffon. I regret that my serious interest in her recipes came too late. Many of them are now lost and will never be made again. I miss her greatly but it is through the few recipes I did write down that she now stands beside me in my kitchen, beaming. And when I make her simple cabbage rolls and sweet tzimmes for my husband, Danny, and my four children, Aunty Myrna joins us at the table.

CHAR-GRILLED ASPARAGUS WITH TOMATO, AVOCADO & HAZELNUT SALAD

Total **45 min;** Serves **8 to 10**

3 pounds asparagus

9 tablespoons extra-virgin olive oil

Sea salt and pepper

⅓ cup raw hazelnuts, coarsely chopped

2 slices of sourdough bread, torn into bite-size pieces (about 3 cups)

2 cups lightly packed flat-leaf parsley leaves, chopped

1 pint multicolored cherry tomatoes, halved

1 ripe Hass avocado, diced

2 tablespoons fresh lemon juice

The Monday Morning Cooking Club loves to serve this salad at barbecues. "The colors, flavors and textures all meld together beautifully," Natanya Eskin says. "The snap of the gorgeous green asparagus, plus rich, creamy avocado with the added crunch from the hazelnuts and croutons—it's a taste of summer and has become one of our favorite salads."

1. Light a grill or heat a grill pan over high heat. In a large bowl, toss the asparagus with 2 tablespoons of the olive oil. Season with salt and pepper. Grill the asparagus in batches until charred but not quite tender, about 2 minutes per side; they will continue to cook as they cool. Transfer to a platter.

2. In a medium skillet, heat 1 tablespoon of the olive oil. Add the hazelnuts and cook over moderate heat, stirring, until golden, 4 minutes. Transfer to a plate.

3. In the same skillet, heat 2 tablespoons of the olive oil. Add the bread and cook over moderate heat, stirring, until golden and crisp, 5 minutes.

4. In a medium bowl, toss the parsley, tomatoes, avocado, croutons, lemon juice and the remaining ¼ cup of olive oil. Season the salad with salt and pepper and spoon over the asparagus. Sprinkle the hazelnuts on top and serve.

FOR MORE ON THE MONDAY MORNING COOKING CLUB

mondaymorningcookingclub.com.au

Monday Morning Cooking Club

@MondayMorningCC

PLENTY MORE

Vibrant Vegetable Cooking from London's Ottolenghi

BY YOTAM OTTOLENGHI

The 2011 release of *Plenty* transformed Jerusalem-born, London-based chef Yotam Ottolenghi into a superstar and stoked an interest in Middle Eastern ingredients that's influenced how many of us eat. Four years in the making, Ottolenghi's similarly vegetable-focused sequel reflects both his latest ingredient obsessions (like black garlic) and a new emphasis on cooking techniques. "Roasting a lemon, for example, or braising lettuce was novel to me a few years ago. Now I am eager to share these ideas," Ottolenghi says. Accordingly, *Plenty More* is organized by method: braised, grilled and so on. These techniques are put to use in dishes like a rice salad with nuts and sour cherries (steamed, p. 218) and a mix of crispy peppers, eggplant and zucchini doused in yogurt and herbed chile oil (fried, p. 222).

Published by Ten Speed Press, $35

RICE SALAD WITH NUTS & SOUR CHERRIES

Serves **6 to 8**

Scant 1 cup/150 g wild rice

Scant 1¼ cups/220 g basmati rice

5½ tbsp/80 ml olive oil

⅔ cup/100 g quinoa

6½ tbsp/60 g almonds, skins on, coarsely chopped

7 tbsp/60 g pine nuts

¼ cup/60 ml sunflower oil

2 medium onions, thinly sliced (about 3 cups/320 g)

1 cup/30 g flat-leaf parsley leaves, coarsely chopped

⅔ cup/20 g basil leaves, coarsely chopped

⅓ cup/10 g tarragon leaves, coarsely chopped

2 cups/40 g arugula

⅔ cup/80 g dried sour cherries

¼ cup/60 ml lemon juice, plus the grated zest of 1 lemon

2 cloves garlic, crushed

Salt and black pepper

Forgive me for all the pots and pans here. They are all left fairly clean, so a good wipe with a towel between uses will save some washing up. The sour cherries have a welcome bite, which sweet raisins lack, so they are worth seeking out in larger shops. You could substitute chopped dried cranberries soaked in a little lemon juice, if need be. This salad makes a satisfying meal-in-a-bowl and will keep in the fridge for a day at least. Just remember not to serve it cold and to readjust the seasoning before serving.

Place the wild rice in a saucepan, cover with plenty of water, bring to a boil, and then turn down to a gentle simmer and cook for 35 minutes, until the rice is cooked but still firm. Drain, rinse under cold water, and set aside to dry.

Mix the basmati rice with 1 tablespoon of the olive oil and ½ teaspoon salt. Place in a saucepan with 1⅓ cups/330 ml of boiling water, cover, and cook over the lowest possible heat for 15 minutes. Remove from the heat, place a tea towel over the pan, replace the lid, and set aside for 10 minutes. Uncover and allow to cool down completely.

Bring a small saucepan of water to a boil and add the quinoa. Cook for 9 minutes, then drain into a fine sieve, refresh under cold water, and set aside.

Place the almonds and pine nuts in a small pan with 1 tablespoon of the olive oil and a pinch of salt. Cook over medium-low heat for about 5 minutes, stirring frequently. Transfer to a small plate as soon as the pine nuts begin to color and set aside.

Heat the sunflower oil in a large sauté pan and add the onions, ¼ teaspoon salt, and some black pepper. Cook over high heat for 5 to 8 minutes, stirring often, so that parts of the onion get crisp and others just soft. Transfer to paper towels to drain.

Place all the grains in a large bowl along with the chopped herbs, arugula, fried onion, nuts, and sour cherries. Add the lemon juice and zest, the remaining 3½ tablespoons olive oil, the garlic, ½ teaspoon salt, and some pepper. Mix well and set aside for at least 10 minutes before serving.

CRUSHED PUY LENTILS WITH TAHINI & CUMIN

Serves **2 as a main course or 4 as a starter**

1 cup/200 g Puy lentils

2 tbsp/30 g unsalted butter

2 tbsp olive oil, plus extra to finish

3 cloves garlic, crushed

1 tsp ground cumin

4 medium tomatoes, peeled and cut into 3/8-inch/1-cm dice (scant 2 cups/330 g)

1 2/3 cups/25 g cilantro leaves, chopped

1/4 cup/60 g tahini paste

2 tbsp lemon juice

1/3 small red onion, thinly sliced (about 1/4 cup/25 g)

2 hard-boiled eggs, quartered

1/2 tsp paprika, to garnish (optional)

Salt and black pepper

EDITOR'S WINE CHOICE
Berry-rich, earthy Pinot Noir.

This recipe has been through various incarnations before ending up uncannily similar to one of the typical Arabic hummus variations I am used to from my childhood: warm hummus topped with whole soft chickpeas and served with raw onion and hard-boiled egg. Here it is made with lentils and tomatoes, but essentially we are talking about a similar set of hearty flavors that can set you up nicely for a busy day, or be served as an early supper. For a dairy-free option, substitute more olive oil for the butter. Serve this with pita and nothing else.

Bring a saucepan of water to a boil. Add the lentils and cook for 20 to 30 minutes, until completely cooked. Drain and set aside.

Put the butter and oil in a large sauté pan and place over medium-high heat. Once the butter melts, add the garlic and cumin and cook for about 1 minute. Add the tomatoes, four-fifths of the cilantro, and the cooked lentils. Continue to cook and stir for a couple of minutes before adding the tahini, lemon juice, 4½ tablespoons/70 ml water, 1 teaspoon salt, and a good grind of black pepper. Lower the heat to medium and continue to stir and cook gently for about 5 minutes, until hot and thickened. Using a potato masher, roughly mash the lentils a little so that some are broken up and you get a thick porridge consistency.

Spread the lentils on a flat serving plate and sprinkle with the onion, the remaining cilantro, and a final drizzle of olive oil. Serve warm with the hard-boiled eggs alongside and a sprinkle of paprika.

MIXED VEGETABLES & YOGURT WITH GREEN CHILE OIL

Serves **4**

3 large plum tomatoes, each cut into 6 wedges (10½ oz/300 g)

Sunflower oil, for frying

2 medium zucchini, cut into ¾-inch/2-cm chunks (about 3 cups/400 g)

1 large eggplant, cut into ¾-inch/2-cm chunks (about 5 cups/450 g)

2 large red peppers, stalks and seeds removed, cut into ¾-inch/2-cm chunks (about 3½ cups/420 g)

¾ cup/150 g Greek yogurt

1 large clove garlic, crushed

1 tbsp shredded fresh mint

1½ tsp dried mint

1½ tsp lemon juice

Salt and black pepper

CHILE AND HERB OIL

1 green chile, coarsely chopped

⅔ oz/20 g flat-leaf parsley

1 tbsp chopped mint

1 tsp ground cumin

¼ cup/60 ml olive oil

Salt

This is a dish I picked up on a visit to Istanbul. I had it in a kebab restaurant, but for me it was actually the vegetables that were the highlight. Try to overlook the fact the vegetables are fried; the dish is still extremely fresh tasting thanks to the yogurt and all the herbs.

Preheat the oven to 325°F/170°C.

Spread out the tomatoes on a baking sheet, sprinkle with ¼ teaspoon salt, and place in the oven for 40 minutes to dry out a little. Remove and set aside to cool.

To make the herb oil, place all the ingredients in the bowl of a small food processor with a pinch of salt and process to a smooth, thick sauce.

Pour the sunflower oil to a depth of 2 inches/5 cm into a saucepan and heat over medium-high heat. Once the oil is hot, turn down the heat to medium. Pat the zucchini and eggplant dry and deep-fry them and the red pepper in batches for 12 to 15 minutes for each. The eggplant might take a little longer than the other vegetables: you want it to be golden brown. Drain in a colander, sprinkle with salt, and set aside to cool.

Finally, in a bowl, stir together the yogurt, garlic, fresh and dried mint, lemon juice, and plenty of black pepper. Add the vegetables and tomatoes and stir very gently. Spoon the herb oil on top and serve.

EDITOR'S WINE CHOICE
Strawberry-scented, vibrant Provençal rosé.

FOR MORE ON YOTAM OTTOLENGHI
ottolenghi.co.uk
Ottolenghi
@ottolenghi

Ben Pollinger shows off the skrei he
caught off the coast of Norway.

PHOTOGRAPH BY ØRJAN BERTELSEN

SCHOOL OF FISH

BY BEN POLLINGER & STEPHANIE LYNESS

Growing up, I never ate fish except fish sticks or tuna casserole," says Ben Pollinger, who, ironically, went on to become one of New York City's premier seafood chefs at Oceana. A swordfish steak shared with his wife-to-be on a date set him on the path to becoming a fish lover. Now he's taken it as his mission to spread the word on how easy and delicious fresh seafood can be. In this fantastic fish primer, he breaks down the techniques and cooking methods, from baking to poaching and grilling, that every home cook needs. Each chapter starts with a "101" level dish, like gazpacho with seared scallops (p. 226), and builds steadily toward more ambitious projects like Spanish chicken, shrimp and rice (p. 230). The practical guide is a textbook—a fun one—for cooks of all levels.

Published by Gallery Books, $35

GAZPACHO 101 WITH SEARED SCALLOPS

Serves **6 as an appetizer (makes about 7 cups)**

- **4** large ripe tomatoes (about 1¾ pounds), cored and coarsely chopped
- **1** large red bell pepper, stem, seeds, and ribs removed, coarsely chopped
- **½** seedless cucumber, peeled and coarsely chopped
- **½** small red onion, coarsely chopped
- **1** clove garlic, coarsely chopped
- **½** red finger chile, cut lengthwise, seeds removed, coarsely chopped
- **¼** cup sherry vinegar
- **1** teaspoon sugar
- Fine sea salt
- **1** teaspoon homemade or store-bought hot sauce
- **¾** cup plus 1 tablespoon extra-virgin olive oil
- **6** large (U15) sea scallops (8 to 10 ounces total), tough white side muscles removed
- Freshly ground black pepper

This chilled bright orange soup makes even not-so-great tomatoes taste good; with better tomatoes, it's stunning. The secret to puréeing this baby is to put the tomatoes into the blender or food processor first. You need their liquid to get the soup moving. Once the vegetables are puréed, drizzle in olive oil to give the soup a rich, creamy consistency. This can be made several days ahead. The soup may separate; just stir it before serving to re-emulsify. And remember that once chilled, the soup will need to be reseasoned.

1. Put the tomatoes in a blender or food processor. Add the bell pepper, cucumber, onion, garlic, chile, vinegar, sugar, 1 tablespoon salt, and the hot sauce. Start the blender on low, if you have a choice of speed. When you see the tomatoes begin to liquefy, turn the blender to high and blend until smooth.

2. With the blender running on medium-high or high speed, drizzle in ¾ cup of the olive oil to emulsify. Transfer to a container, cover, and refrigerate until well chilled.

3. When you're ready to serve, sprinkle the scallops on both sides with salt and pepper and let stand 5 minutes to allow the seasonings to penetrate.

4. Taste the soup for seasoning. It may have separated: stir until smooth.

5. Place a skillet over medium heat. Add the remaining 1 tablespoon olive oil and heat until it shimmers. Remove the pan from the heat to avoid flare-ups and gently lay the scallops in the pan, placing the edge closest to you down first so as not to splatter yourself with hot oil. Return the pan to the heat and cook until the scallops are a nice golden color on the pan side and the bottom third of the scallop is opaque, about 2 minutes. Carefully turn the scallops with a spatula and cook until the other side is golden brown and the scallops are medium-rare with all but the center third opaque, 1 to 2 minutes depending on size.

6. Center a scallop in the bottom of each of six shallow serving bowls. Pour the soup into a large measuring cup. Pour the soup around the scallops so that the scallops are visible.

EXTRA CREDIT: GAZPACHO GARNISH

For a more formal restaurant-style presentation that also gives the soup texture, peel and quarter a 3-inch chunk of seedless cucumber; cut into ⅛-inch dice. Very finely dice (⅛ inch) enough red bell pepper to make 6 tablespoons. Cut three 1-inch wedges of tomato and cut out the core and seeds; cut the flesh into ⅛-inch dice. Combine the vegetables in a small bowl with 1 tablespoon extra-virgin olive oil, a pinch each of salt and black pepper, and 3 tablespoons slivered fresh cilantro. To serve, spoon this mixture into the serving bowls before adding the scallops.

EDITOR'S WINE CHOICE
Bold, robustly fruity Spanish rosé.

SALMON BURGERS WITH PICKLED RED ONIONS & HORSERADISH AIOLI

Serves **4 as an entrée**

FOR THE PICKLED RED ONIONS

- 2 **medium red onions, sliced crosswise into thin rounds**
- 2 **cups red wine vinegar**
- 1 **cup sugar**

FOR THE HORSERADISH AIOLI

- 1 **cup homemade or good-quality store-bought mayonnaise**
- 1 **tablespoon plus 1 teaspoon white prepared horseradish, excess liquid pressed out with clean fingers**

FOR THE SALMON BURGERS

- 2 **pounds boneless, skinless salmon fillet, pin bones removed**
- **Fine sea salt and freshly ground black pepper**
- 1 **teaspoon canola oil**
- 4 **hamburger buns**
- 2 **tablespoons unsalted butter, softened or melted**
- 1 **cup loosely packed arugula leaves, for serving**

I make this with wild coho salmon, which has a full, meaty flavor and it cooks up with a bright orange color. Coho is lean, however, so if you use it, be particularly careful to cook the burgers to medium-rare or they will be dry. Otherwise, farm-raised salmon is a fine substitute and the texture is more forgiving than coho. If you have the time, the onions are best made the day before.

1. For the onions, place in a heatproof bowl. In a small saucepan, bring the vinegar and sugar to a boil, stirring occasionally to dissolve the sugar. Pour over the onions—they should be entirely submerged (choose a smaller container, if necessary). Cover and let stand at least 1 hour or overnight to cool completely to room temperature. Set aside.

2. For the aioli, whisk the mayonnaise with the horseradish in a bowl. Refrigerate until you're ready to serve.

3. For the burgers, if you have a grinder attachment for your standing mixer, cut the salmon into long strips and chill the salmon and the grinder attachment and small-hole plate in the freezer for 15 minutes. Grind the salmon into a chilled bowl. Or cut the salmon into small dice and chill in the freezer for 15 minutes along with the bowl and blade of the food processor. Pulse until coarsely ground. Do not overwork. Shape the ground salmon into 4 equal patties about 3½ inches in diameter. Place on a plate, cover, and refrigerate.

4. Preheat a gas grill to high. Scrub the grill grates with a grill brush. Season the patties on both sides with salt and pepper. Brush each side with ¼ teaspoon canola oil.

5. Oil the grill grates. Place the burgers on the grill over high heat and cook 1½ minutes to mark. Turn 90 degrees with a spatula to make a crosshatch pattern and cook 1½ minutes more. Flip the patties with the spatula and cook 1½ minutes more. Turn 90 degrees with the spatula and grill until the burgers are cooked to medium-rare, about 1½ minutes more.

6. Lightly rub the cut sides of the buns with the butter. Reduce the heat on one zone of the grill to medium-low. Toast the buns over medium-low heat until marked, 30 to 45 seconds. Turn 90 degrees with a spatula to make a crosshatch pattern and toast about 30 seconds more.

7. Serve the burgers in the buns with the aioli, onions, and arugula.

**EDITOR'S
WINE CHOICE**
Lightly oaked,
full-bodied
Chardonnay.

CRISTINA'S SPANISH CHICKEN, SHRIMP & RICE

Serves **4 generously as an entrée**

- 1 **pound boneless, skinless chicken thighs, cut into ½-inch dice**
- 3 **cloves garlic, peeled**
- 1 **tablespoon slivered fresh Italian parsley**
- 4 **tablespoons extra-virgin olive oil**
- 1 **pound small or medium (31–40 or 21–30) shrimp, shelled, tails removed, deveined**
- 1 **cup chopped onion (about 1 medium)**
- ½ **cup chopped red bell pepper (about ¼ pepper)**
- ½ **cup chopped fresh tomatoes (about 1 medium)**
- ½ **cup dry white wine**
- ½ **cup homemade clam broth or bottled clam juice**
- ⅛ **teaspoon saffron threads**
- 1 **bay leaf**
- 3 **cups homemade chicken stock or store-bought low-sodium chicken stock**
-    **Fine sea salt**
- 1½ **cups basmati rice**

I owe this recipe to Cristina Mosquera, a friend of the family and a fantastic Spanish cook. I always look forward to dinner when she cooks, as much for the food as for the company. From the spread she and her husband, Victor, set out for us you'd think she was cooking for an army. This is one of my favorites. If it's more convenient, make the dish up to an hour ahead, cover with foil, and hold in a warm oven. When you're ready to serve, heat ½ cup stock and stir it in to moisten the rice.

1. Place the chicken in a medium bowl or baking dish. Chop 2 of the garlic cloves and add to the chicken along with the parsley and 1 tablespoon of the olive oil. Toss to coat the chicken; cover with plastic wrap and set aside at room temperature (see Kitchen Notebook: Prevent Sticking, opposite).

2. Place the shrimp in another medium bowl or baking dish and toss with 1 tablespoon of the olive oil; cover with plastic wrap and set aside at room temperature.

3. Place a 10-inch skillet over medium-low heat. Add 1 tablespoon of olive oil and heat until fluid enough to coat the bottom of the pan when swirled. Add the onion and the remaining whole garlic clove. Cook without coloring, stirring often, until the onion is tender and translucent, about 5 minutes.

4. Add the bell pepper and cook without coloring, stirring often, until tender, about 4 minutes more.

5. Add the tomato and cook, stirring occasionally, until it has softened and begun to break down, about 5 minutes.

6. Add the wine, clam broth or clam juice, saffron, bay leaf, 1 cup of the chicken stock, and ½ teaspoon salt. Simmer, uncovered, to allow the flavors to meld, 6 to 7 minutes.

7. Add the rice, stir, and then simmer without stirring, uncovered, for 5 minutes.

8. Add another 1 cup of the chicken stock and stir gently. Simmer 5 minutes more, until the liquid has been mostly absorbed (the pan will not be dry).

9. Add another ½ cup chicken stock, stir gently, and continue cooking until the rice is tender and the stock has been almost completely absorbed, about 10 minutes more. Keep in mind that the rice will continue to absorb liquid after you've removed it from the heat; make sure some liquid remains or the rice will be dry. Add a bit more, if necessary. Fish out and discard the bay leaf.

10. About 5 minutes into the previous step, heat a 12-inch skillet over high heat. Add the remaining 1 tablespoon olive oil and heat until it shimmers. Add the chicken in a single layer. Let it brown without stirring, 1 minute. Season with ½ teaspoon salt, stir, and cook 1 minute more. Stir in the shrimp. Cook 1 minute more. Remove from the heat and set aside until the rice is done.

11. Add the chicken and shrimp to the rice. Pour the remaining ½ cup chicken stock into the pan in which the chicken and shrimp were cooked and let stand off the heat for 1 minute to soften the browned bits on the bottom of the pan. Scrape up the browned bits with a spatula or wooden spoon and pour with the liquid into the rice. Stir to combine. Serve from the pan in which the rice was cooked.

KITCHEN NOTEBOOK: PREVENT STICKING

Room-temperature meat and seafood are less likely to stick to the pan while cooking. They won't lower the temperature of the pan significantly, so they will develop a crust more quickly. So it makes sense to bring the shrimp and chicken to room temperature while you cook the rice.

EDITOR'S WINE CHOICE
Juicy, medium-bodied Spanish white, such as Verdejo.

FILLET OF FLOUNDER 101 MEUNIÈRE

Serves **2 as an entrée**

14 to 16 ounces boneless, skinless fluke fillets

Fine sea salt and freshly ground black pepper

¼ cup all-purpose flour

3 tablespoons canola oil

2 teaspoons plus 3 tablespoons unsalted butter

¼ cup gently packed slivered fresh Italian parsley

2¼ teaspoons fresh lemon juice

This is your basic technique for sautéing any thin flatfish fillet such as flounder, fluke, gray sole, lemon sole, and petrale sole. I flour the fillets and add a little butter about halfway through cooking for better browning and flavor. The classic recipe (called meunière, *meaning "miller's wife" because the fish is coated in flour) is sauced with nut-brown butter, lemon juice, and parsley, but you can change the flavor profile with lime, orange, or even yuzu juice. As far as accompaniments for a meunière preparation, you want to keep it simple so as not to distract from the delicate flavor of the lemon and brown butter.*

1. Pat the fillets dry with paper towels. On a baking sheet, sprinkle one side of each fillet with salt and pepper. Let stand a few minutes to allow the seasonings to penetrate. Line a baking sheet with paper towels to drain the fish.

2. Spread the flour over a plate. Dredge the fillets in the flour, flipping them a few times and patting the flour over the fillets to create an even, thin layer.

3. Place a 12-inch skillet over high heat. Add the oil and heat until it shimmers and almost smokes. Gently shake off the excess flour and gently lay the floured fillets side by side in the pan, placing the edge closest to you down first so as not to splatter yourself with hot oil, and allowing a little space between them. (Larger fillets will fit best in the center of the pan; smaller fillets on the sides.) Cook for about 1 minute to allow the crust to form, then turn the heat down to medium-high. Cook until the fillets are golden brown and are opaque around the edges, about 1 minute more. Add the 2 teaspoons butter to the pan, swirl gently to melt, and cook 1 minute more.

4. Turn the heat down to medium. Flip the fillets gently with a spatula and cook until the fillets are cooked through, 2 to 3 minutes more. Remove the fillets to the paper towel–lined baking sheet.

5. Drain the fat from the pan and wipe out the pan if there are any burned bits on the bottom. Otherwise, add the remaining 3 tablespoons butter to the pan and heat over medium heat, swirling, 15 to 30 seconds. The butter will be foamy and as the foam subsides, the butter will begin to turn a golden brown color. Remove from the heat. Add the parsley, lemon juice, and ⅛ teaspoon salt and swirl to combine.

6. Divide the fillets between two serving plates, overlapping the fillets on each plate. Spoon the sauce over.

KITCHEN NOTEBOOK: CUT TO FIT
Your fillets are probably going to be different sizes and shapes. Cut them as needed so that you have two relatively equal portions.

**EDITOR'S
WINE CHOICE**
Vibrant,
minerally
Muscadet.

Ben Pollinger sources black sea bass, his favorite fish, from Fulton Fish Market in New York City.

STEAMED BLACK SEA BASS WITH CARROT-LIME SAUCE

Total **1 hr 30 min**; Serves **4**

Ben Pollinger's favorite fish dish is black sea bass steamed with the skin on. "It's very supple, with great flavor and texture—not too firm but not too flaky," he says. He drizzles the fish with a light but luscious carrot-lime sauce scented with lemongrass; the sauce would be excellent with any white fish steamed, seared or roasted.

CARROT-LIME SAUCE

- 1 tablespoon canola oil
- One 1-inch piece of lemongrass, smashed
- 1 small shallot, sliced
- 2 medium carrots, sliced
- Kosher salt
- ¼ cup fresh lime juice

VEGETABLES

- 8 fingerling potatoes, scrubbed
- 2 tablespoons extra-virgin olive oil
- 8 baby carrots, scrubbed
- 8 baby turnips, scrubbed
- Kosher salt and black pepper
- 12 sugar snap peas
- ¼ cup chicken stock or water
- 2 tablespoons chopped chives
- 8 basil leaves, torn

STEAMED FISH

- Four 7-ounce black sea bass fillets with skin
- Kosher salt and black pepper
- 2 teaspoons extra-virgin olive oil
- 1 small shallot, minced
- 1 small jalapeño—halved, seeded and thinly sliced

EDITOR'S WINE CHOICE
Citrusy, medium-bodied Sauvignon Blanc, such as Sancerre.

1. Make the carrot-lime sauce In a small saucepan, heat the canola oil. Add the lemongrass and cook over moderately low heat until fragrant, about 30 seconds. Add the shallot and cook, stirring, until softened, about 5 minutes. Add the carrot slices and season with salt. Cook over moderate heat, stirring, until the carrots are just tender, about 6 minutes. Add the lime juice and 2 cups of water and bring to a boil. Simmer over moderate heat, stirring occasionally, until the carrots are soft, about 20 minutes. Discard the lemongrass and transfer the contents of the pan to a blender. Puree until smooth. Season the sauce with salt.

2. Prepare the vegetables In a medium saucepan of salted boiling water, cook the potatoes over moderately high heat until tender, 10 to 12 minutes. Drain well. Meanwhile, in a large skillet, heat the olive oil. Add the baby carrots and turnips and season with salt and pepper. Cover and cook over moderate heat, stirring occasionally, until tender, 12 to 15 minutes. Add the cooked potatoes, the snap peas and the chicken stock and cook until hot, about 2 minutes. Stir in the chives and basil.

3. Steam the fish In a large wok or pot, bring about 2 inches of water to a boil over high heat. Cut a piece of parchment paper to fit a large bamboo or metal steamer basket. Cut several slits in the paper to allow steam to pass through. Place the fish on the parchment and season with salt and pepper. Drizzle with the olive oil and top with the shallot and chile. Carefully put the fish (and paper) in the steamer. Cover and steam over moderately high heat until the fish is white throughout, about 8 minutes.

4. Arrange the vegetables on plates and drizzle with the carrot-lime sauce. Set the fillets on top, skin side down, and serve.

FOR MORE ON BEN POLLINGER
oceanarestaurant.com
f Oceana Restaurant
🐦 @benpollinger

Marcus Samuelsson in Harlem, where he lives in a brownstone that was once home to rapper Heavy D and basketball legend Kareem Abdul-Jabbar.

MARCUS OFF DUTY

The Recipes I Cook at Home

BY MARCUS SAMUELSSON WITH ROY FINAMORE

Many chefs don't have the time or energy to cook at home (they can barely stock the fridge with beer), but Marcus Samuelsson is the exception. In this book, the mega-talent behind the global soul food at Harlem's Red Rooster shares the recipes he makes for his wife and their friends. These reflect his fascinating life story: "I start as an Ethiopian raised in Sweden and trained in French techniques, but I bring the flavors of many cultures to my table." Mexico, Southeast Asia, the Caribbean, New Orleans, Manhattan's Koreatown—Samuelsson is omnivorous. His Salmon in a Sea of Coconut (p. 238) combines Sweden's signature fish and dill with coconut milk, miso and Chinese noodles. His cheater's version of Texas brisket (p. 240) comes with a delicious and highly inauthentic sauce spiced with fresh ginger. "I understand that I belong in a kitchen at home," he writes. "And I have homes in many places."

Published by Houghton Mifflin Harcourt, $35

SALMON IN A SEA OF COCONUT

Serves **4**

3 tablespoons olive oil

3 ounces shiitake mushrooms, stemmed and sliced (about 1 cup)

2 shallots, sliced

1 teaspoon grated peeled ginger

2 cups fish stock

1 cup coconut milk

1 tablespoon dry white wine

1 tablespoon white miso

4 ounces Chinese egg noodles (fresh or dried)

Juice of 1 lime

4 scallions, sliced

½ cup canned drained water chestnuts, coarsely chopped (see Note)

2 canned hearts of palm, well rinsed and sliced (see Note)

½ ripe avocado, diced into small pieces

Kosher salt

1 pound skinless salmon fillet, cut into 4 pieces

½ tablespoon wasabi powder (see Note)

1 tablespoon sesame seeds

2 teaspoons chopped fresh mint

2 teaspoons chopped fresh dill

**EDITOR'S
BEER CHOICE**
Crisp, lightly
hoppy ale, such
as Kölsch.

Growing up on the west coast of Sweden, I was lucky enough to have access to some of the best salmon in the world, which I would catch with my father sometimes. But I think if I was told that I could eat the food of one region only for the rest of my life, it would be the cuisines of Southeast Asia. So this recipe highlights my salmon, but I also turn to coconut milk, fresh ginger, and white miso. Weirdly delicious water chestnuts add a hint of bitterness and crunch and the hearts of palm contribute a meaty chew.

1. Heat 2 tablespoons of the olive oil in a large pot over medium heat. When the oil shimmers, add the mushrooms, shallots, and ginger and cook until the mushrooms are just tender and starting to brown, about 6 minutes. Add the fish stock, coconut milk, white wine, and miso and bring to a boil. Stir in the noodles, reduce the heat to low, and cook until just tender, 4 to 5 minutes.

2. Stir in the lime juice, scallions, water chestnuts, hearts of palm, and avocado. Season with salt (start with ½ teaspoon salt and add more carefully to keep from overpowering the delicate flavors). Turn off the heat, cover the pot, and keep warm.

3. Sprinkle the skinned side of the salmon with the wasabi and sesame seeds. Heat the remaining 1 tablespoon olive oil in a large skillet over medium-high heat and add the salmon fillets, skin side down. You'll see the salmon change color as it cooks from the bottom. When it is still rare, 3 to 4 minutes, flip the fillets so the heat can kiss the top of the fish. Turn off the heat.

4. Spoon the noodles and soup into four soup bowls, then top each serving with a piece of salmon and sprinkle with the chopped mint and dill.

NOTES

• *You can find canned water chestnuts and hearts of palm in most grocery stores.*

• *Wasabi powder is in the Asian section of most grocery stores. Check the label to make sure it's wasabi—not horseradish and food coloring.*

SPICE-RUBBED TEXAS BRISKET FROM THE OVEN

Serves **6 to 8**

FOR THE SPICE RUB

- 1 **tablespoon chile powder**
- 1 **teaspoon smoked paprika**
- 1 **teaspoon kosher salt**
- ½ **teaspoon ground cumin**
- ½ **teaspoon dried sage, crumbled**
- ½ **teaspoon sugar**
- ½ **teaspoon ground oregano**
- ¼ **teaspoon cayenne**
- ¼ **teaspoon freshly ground black pepper**

FOR THE BRISKET

- 2 **large garlic cloves, minced**
- **One 5-pound beef brisket, flat cut**
- **Barbecue Sauce (recipe follows)**

Texas is one of my favorite places to cook—and eat. There's nothing like Texas barbecued brisket. But smoking a piece of beef for hours isn't the easiest thing, so I rub the meat with chile powder, smoked paprika, cumin, sage, and oregano, wrap it tightly in foil, and roast it low and slow for a brisket that's moist and succulent and packed with smoky spice. The sweet tanginess of the barbecue sauce, which has a little heat from the chipotles and ginger, is the perfect accompaniment.

You could serve this with spongy sliced white bread like they do in Texas. Sometimes something so wrong can be so right.

1. Preheat the oven to 325°F.

2. Make the spice rub Mix the seasonings together in a small bowl.

3. Make the brisket Rub the garlic into both sides of the brisket, then rub in the spice rub. Set the brisket, fat side up, on two large overlapping pieces of heavy-duty foil. Wrap the brisket tightly in the foil and set it on a rimmed baking sheet. Roast until tender, about 3 hours. Serve hot or cold with warm barbecue sauce.

Barbecue Sauce

You can make this up to 1 week ahead. Keep it covered in the refrigerator, but heat it before serving. It's great with the brisket, but try serving it with chicken or pork meatballs. Even with roasted vegetables.

Melt 1 tablespoon unsalted butter in a medium saucepan over medium heat. Add 2 minced garlic cloves and cook until fragrant, about 1 minute. Stir in ½ cup ketchup, ½ cup canned crushed tomatoes, ½ cup packed light brown sugar, ½ cup red wine vinegar, ¼ cup fresh lemon juice, 2 tablespoons Worcestershire sauce, 2 chopped chipotles in adobo, 2 teaspoons mustard seeds, 1 teaspoon grated fresh ginger, and a pinch of cayenne.

Bring the sauce to a boil. Reduce the heat to medium-low and simmer, stirring occasionally, until the sauce is thickened and reduced to about 1½ cups, 15 to 20 minutes. Give it a taste and season with salt and pepper.

EDITOR'S WINE CHOICE
Robust, smoky Washington state Syrah.

STEAMED CATFISH WITH CITRUS-SOY VINAIGRETTE

Serves **4**

FOR THE VINAIGRETTE

- 1 garlic clove, minced
- One 1-inch piece ginger, peeled and grated
- Zest and juice of 1 lime
- Zest and juice of 1 orange
- 2 tablespoons soy sauce
- 1 teaspoon sesame oil
- ½ teaspoon fish sauce
- ½ teaspoon sugar
- 2 tablespoons olive oil

FOR THE FISH

- Four 6-ounce catfish fillets
- Peels from the garlic and ginger
- Shells from the lime and orange
- Coarse sea salt

AUTHOR'S NOTE
Save the lime and orange shells and the ginger and garlic peels when you prep the vinaigrette and drop them into the steaming liquid for the fish. They all add flavor.

EDITOR'S WINE CHOICE
Lime-scented, dry Australian Riesling.

Catfish is like an old jazz standard. It's familiar—and you think you're kind of tired of it. Then you hear someone play it in an entirely new way, and you remember that it's a standard not because someone famous wrote it, or because someone famous sang it. It's a standard because, at the heart of it, there's something universal and true and good. Catfish has been part of the home cook's repertoire for hundreds of years. It's as popular in Europe and Asia as it is in North America and Africa.

My favorite way to prepare catfish is to steam it. Steaming is quick, and it adds some elegance to this common fish. (You can buy a stack-and-steam pot or a bamboo steamer in most kitchenware stores, Chinese markets, and online.) But what really sets this recipe apart is the citrus-soy vinaigrette; it infuses the delicate fillets with a bright, slightly spicy, Asian flavor.

1. Make the vinaigrette Put all the ingredients except the olive oil in a jar, cover, and shake vigorously. Strain the solids through a fine-mesh sieve. Reserve the solids and liquid.

2. Heat the olive oil in a small saucepan over medium-low heat. Add the solids and cook until the garlic is fragrant, 1 to 2 minutes. Add the reserved liquid, bring to a boil, and cook for 1 minute. Set aside to cool.

3. Steam the fish Place 1 inch of water in the bottom of a steamer, along with ginger and garlic peels, lime and orange shells, and sea salt to taste. Cover the steamer and bring the water to a boil. Remove the lid, lay the fish on the steamer racks, making sure the rack is elevated above the water, and cover. Steam until the fish is opaque and flaky, about 4 minutes.

4. To serve, plate the fish and drizzle with the vinaigrette.

THE FARM GIRL SALAD

Active **25 min**; Total **1 hr**; Serves **4**

At his Harlem restaurant Streetbird Rotisserie, Marcus Samuelsson serves eclectic dishes with global influences like this kale and green bean salad. He gives the recipe a Southeast Asian spin with a coconut-lime dressing and nutty toasted rice—a traditional topping for Thai salads.

TOASTED RICE

- ½ **cup raw white rice**
- 1 **garlic clove, sliced**
- **One 1-inch piece of lemongrass bulb, smashed**
- **One ½-inch piece of fresh ginger, peeled and thinly sliced**
- 1 **teaspoon light brown sugar**
- **Kosher salt**

COCONUT-LIME DRESSING

- 2 **tablespoons coconut cream (see Note)**
- 2 **tablespoons fresh lime juice**
- 1 **tablespoon honey**
- 2½ **teaspoons hot sauce**
- ¼ **teaspoon Dijon mustard**
- 2 **tablespoons grapeseed oil**
- 1½ **teaspoons extra-virgin olive oil**
- **Kosher salt and pepper**

SALAD

- 4 **ounces green beans, halved**
- ¾ **pound romaine lettuce, cut into 1½-inch pieces (6 cups)**
- ¾ **pound Tuscan kale, stemmed, leaves chopped into ½-inch pieces (4 cups)**
- **Kosher salt**

1. Toast the rice Preheat the oven to 300°F. On a small rimmed baking sheet, toss the rice with the garlic, lemongrass and ginger. Bake until golden brown, stirring once, 20 to 25 minutes. Remove and let cool. Discard the garlic, lemongrass and ginger. Transfer the toasted rice to a blender or mini food processor and blend until finely ground. Sift through a fine strainer and discard any big grains. Stir in the sugar and season with salt.

2. Make the dressing In a blender, combine the coconut cream, lime juice, honey, hot sauce and mustard. Puree, then slowly add the grapeseed oil and olive oil until emulsified. Season with salt and pepper.

3. Make the salad Fill a medium bowl with ice water. In a medium saucepan of boiling water, blanch the green beans for 1 minute. Drain, then transfer to the ice water to cool. Drain well and pat dry.

4. In a large bowl, toss the green beans with the lettuce, kale and dressing. Season with salt. Sprinkle with the toasted rice and serve.

NOTE Coconut cream is four times richer than coconut milk. It is sold in cans and can also be skimmed from the thick, rich cream that rises to the top of a can of coconut milk.

FOR MORE ON MARCUS SAMUELSSON
marcussamuelsson.com
 Marcus Samuelsson
 @MarcusCooks

Mimi Thorisson (here, with daughter Gaïa) runs cooking workshops out of her villa in Médoc.

A KITCHEN IN FRANCE

A Year of Cooking in My Farmhouse

BY MIMI THORISSON

In the dreamy world of Mimi Thorisson, the kitchen table is a tableau of ingredients in color-saturated hues and life revolves around rituals like foraging for mushrooms in the forest. Thorisson, creator of the blog Manger and star of the TV show *La Table de Mimi*, shares her seasonal cooking repertoire and tells stories about life in Bordeaux with her photographer husband, Oddur, their children and purebred terriers. Her recipes prove that elegant French cooking is a daily possibility—whether that means topping mussels with herbs and ground almonds (p. 246) or dusting lemony brioche dough with sugar for a delectable, caramelized crust (p. 250). "If I can inspire people to cook good food with high-quality ingredients, using simple everyday French recipes, I will have achieved something," Thorisson states.

Published by Clarkson Potter, $40

ALMOND MUSSELS

Serves **4 to 6**

1 cup/60 g fresh bread crumbs

7 tablespoons/80 g unsalted butter, at room temperature

A bunch of fresh parsley, leaves removed and finely chopped

3 garlic cloves, minced

Fine sea salt and freshly ground black pepper

1½ cups/180 g finely ground almonds

4 pounds/2 kg mussels, scrubbed if necessary

When I am shopping for mussels, somehow a line from Oscar Wilde's The Importance of Being Earnest *always pops into my head, reminding me to get them when they look pretty and to skip them when they don't. (The quote is much more apt when applied to mussels than women, in my mind.) That leaves how to prepare them.* Moules marinière *is as classic as any dish in France (or Belgium), lovely with French fries. When I am in Normandy, having them with cream is a must. At home, I seem to make them most often with sausage meat or, as in this case, with almonds. This version makes a nice starter; I place a big baking dish of them on the table outside and guests can nibble on the mussels while sipping crisp white wine and awaiting the next course.*

Combine the bread crumbs, butter, parsley, and garlic in a bowl, season with salt and pepper, and mix well. Mix in the almonds. The mixture will have the consistency of a paste.

Preheat the oven to 425°F/220°C.

Put the mussels in a large pot, cover, and cook over high heat until they just open, a few minutes. Remove from the heat, uncover, and let cool slightly.

Discard any mussels that did not open. Remove one half shell from each mussel, and arrange them mussel-side up in a shallow baking dish. Scoop about ½ teaspoon of the stuffing onto each mussel. Season with salt and pepper.

Transfer the baking dish to the oven and bake until the surface of the mussels is golden and bubbly, about 6 minutes. Serve immediately.

EDITOR'S WINE CHOICE
Crisp, fragrant white Bordeaux.

BLANQUETTE DE VEAU

Serves **6**

- 2½ pounds/1 kg boneless veal shoulder, cut into 2-inch/5-cm cubes
- 2 small shallots
- 4 cloves
- 2 carrots, peeled and cut into chunks
- 2 leeks, white part only, sliced
- 1 celery stalk, sliced
- 1 small onion, sliced
- 2 garlic cloves, sliced
- 1 bouquet garni [1 bay leaf and 2 sprigs each of thyme and parsley tied with kitchen string]
- ¼ cup/60 ml dry white wine, optional
- Fine sea salt
- 6 tablespoons/90 g unsalted butter
- ⅓ cup/40 g all-purpose flour
- Freshly ground black pepper
- 8 ounces/250 g white mushrooms, sliced
- 5 ounces/150 g pearl onions, peeled
- Juice of 1 lemon
- ⅔ cup/160 ml crème fraîche
- 2 large egg yolks
- A handful of chopped fresh parsley

EDITOR'S WINE CHOICE
Concentrated, earthy white Burgundy.

If I were asked what the quintessential French dish is, I would be tempted to say blanquette de veau. *I've been having it for as long as I can remember. It's often incredibly aromatic and subtly delicious, but even somewhat bland versions somehow always seem heartwarming. It's one of the foods I find most soothing and comforting. I can't think of a more typical example of bourgeois cooking—meat and vegetables slowly uniting in a tasty winter stew, served over boiled potatoes or rice. It's the sort of old-fashioned dish I think deserves another look.*

Bring a large pot of salted water, enough to generously cover the meat, to a boil. Add the veal, return to a boil, and cook for 1 minute. Skim any scum from the surface.

Meanwhile, slice 1½ of the shallots. Stick the cloves into the remaining ½ shallot. Add the carrots, leeks, celery, onion, garlic, all the shallots, and the bouquet garni to the pot, then add the wine, bring to a low boil, and cook for 2 minutes. Season with 1 tablespoon salt, cover, and simmer over low heat until the veal is tender, about 1 hour and 15 minutes.

Strain the meat and vegetables from the broth and set aside. Discard the bouquet garni. Reserve the broth in the pot.

Melt 4 tablespoons/60 g of the butter in a small saucepan over medium heat. Add the flour, whisking constantly, and cook, stirring until the roux thickens, about 2 minutes. Season with salt and pepper. Pour the roux into the pot with the broth, whisking constantly, and simmer over low heat until the broth starts to thicken slightly, about 5 minutes.

Return the meat and vegetables to the pot, cover, and simmer for 15 minutes.

Meanwhile, heat the remaining 2 tablespoons/30 g of butter in a medium sauté pan over medium heat. Cook the mushrooms and pearl onions until golden, about 6 minutes. Drizzle in half of the lemon juice and simmer for 30 seconds. Add to the big pot.

In a small bowl, mix together the crème fraîche and the remaining lemon juice, then whisk in the egg yolks. Add a ladle or two of the cooking liquid, whisk well, and pour the mixture into the big pot. (Do not boil, or the egg and cream will curdle.)

Remove from the heat and serve immediately, garnished with the parsley.

GALETTE PÉROUGIENNE

Serves **4 to 6**

2 teaspoons active dry yeast

⅓ cup/80 ml lukewarm water

12 tablespoons/1½ sticks/ 180 g unsalted butter, plus more for the bowl, at room temperature

1 large egg

Grated zest of 1 lemon

Pinch of fine sea salt

½ cup/100 g granulated sugar

1⅓ cups/160 g all-purpose flour, sifted, plus more for rolling

This is a wonderful specialty from the medieval town of Pérouges, near Lyon, made from a lemony yeasted brioche dough that is sprinkled with a generous amount of sugar, dotted with butter, and baked in a very hot oven. The sugar caramelizes and each bite is a pure delight. I am very fond of this medieval cake. It is so authentic and simple in taste—exactly what I look for in a dessert.

Mix the yeast in the lukewarm water in a small cup. Set aside for 5 minutes to allow the yeast to dissolve.

In a large bowl, mix together 8 tablespoons/120 g of the butter with the egg, lemon zest, salt, and 2 tablespoons of the sugar. Add the yeast mixture and then gradually add the flour, mixing with a wooden spoon until you have a soft and elastic dough.

Shape the dough into a ball, put it in a buttered bowl, cover with a damp cloth, and let rise in a warm spot until doubled in size, at least 2 hours.

Preheat the oven to 450°F/230°C. Line a baking sheet with parchment paper.

On a parchment-paper-lined surface, roll the dough into a 9-inch/23-cm circle about ½ inch/1 cm thick. Press on the edges to make a ½-inch/ 1-cm-wide raised border. Sprinkle the remaining 6 tablespoons/75 g sugar over the dough and dot with the remaining 4 tablespoons/60 g butter.

Transfer to the baking sheet and bake until golden and caramelized, 15 minutes. Let cool for 5 minutes and serve warm.

SERRANO-WRAPPED COD WITH SAUCE BASQUE

Active **40 min**; Total **1 hr 15 min**; Serves **6**

1¾ pounds tomatoes

¼ cup extra-virgin olive oil

½ pound yellow onions, thinly sliced

3 garlic cloves, sliced

1 cup jarred piquillo peppers, drained and thinly sliced

1 tablespoon tomato paste

1 thyme sprig

1 bay leaf

½ teaspoon piment d'Espelette

Kosher salt and pepper

Six 5-ounce skinless cod fillets

6 thin slices of serrano ham

2 tablespoons chopped chives

"Basque cuisine is so tasty, highly influenced by seafood, cured hams, tomatoes and peppers," Mimi Thorisson says. "It's my kind of rustic food." Here, she simmers a simple Basque-style sauce to pair with cod fillets wrapped in serrano ham, then seared until crisp. "The ham perfumes the fish in all the right ways, and when you add a bite of the 'very red ratatouille' (that's what the kids call it), it's simply delicious."

1. Score the bottoms of the tomatoes with a small X. In a medium saucepan of boiling water, blanch the tomatoes until the skins start to peel back, about 3 minutes. Remove the tomatoes and let cool slightly, then peel and coarsely chop them.

2. In a medium saucepan, heat 2 tablespoons of the olive oil. Add the onions and garlic and cook over moderate heat, stirring occasionally, until the onions are softened, about 5 minutes. Add the piquillos and cook for 3 minutes. Add the chopped tomatoes, the tomato paste, thyme sprig, bay leaf and piment d'Espelette. Season with salt and pepper, cover and cook, stirring occasionally, until saucy, about 30 minutes. Discard the thyme sprig and bay leaf.

3. Season the fish with salt and pepper and wrap each fillet in a slice of serrano ham. In a large skillet, heat the remaining 2 tablespoons of olive oil. Add the fillets and cook over moderately high heat until the ham is crisp and the fish is cooked through, 3 to 4 minutes per side. Serve the fish on the sauce, topped with the chives.

EDITOR'S WINE CHOICE
Fruit-forward, medium-bodied white Bordeaux.

FOR MORE ON MIMI THORISSON
mimithorisson.com
⬛ Manger by Mimi Thorisson

MY PERFECT PANTRY

150 Easy Recipes from 50 Essential Ingredients

BY GEOFFREY ZAKARIAN WITH AMY STEVENSON & MARGARET ZAKARIAN

Geoffrey Zakarian, the Food Network star and chef and co-owner of The Lambs Club in New York City, believes that although green-market ingredients get all the attention, "the real engine of the kitchen is the pantry." He guarantees that the 50 ingredients he focuses on in his new book can "fuel an array of American meals, morning through night." He offers three simple recipes for each of the essential items, which range from almonds and yeast to the Earl Grey tea bags he steeps in syrup for French toast (p. 260). He also suggests clever uses for leftovers: Brown rice, for instance, is the stealth ingredient in crisp crab cakes (p. 256). Zakarian considers every aspect of pantry maintenance, including shelf life (confectioners' sugar keeps indefinitely)—information that helps you make the most of your larder. "This book will unlock all your other cookbooks," he says.

Published by Clarkson Potter, $30

BROWN RICE CRAB CAKES

Makes **8 crab cakes**

1 pound jumbo lump crabmeat, picked over for shells

½ cup mayonnaise

¾ cup cooled cooked brown rice

½ cup chopped scallions (white and green parts)

1 large egg, beaten

Finely grated zest and juice of 1 lemon (about 3 tablespoons juice)

1 tablespoon chopped fresh tarragon

Kosher salt and freshly ground black pepper

1¼ cups fine dry bread crumbs, plus more as needed

Canola oil, for frying

1 lemon, cut into wedges, for serving

EDITOR'S WINE CHOICE
Apple-scented, lightly oaked California Chardonnay.

Leftover brown rice helps stretch a pound of crab into eight good-size crab cakes. I get the best results with cooked rice that has first been spread on a plate and chilled in the refrigerator, which dries it out a bit.

1. In a large bowl, combine the crab, mayonnaise, rice, scallions, egg, lemon zest and juice, and tarragon. Stir to combine. Season with salt and pepper. Sprinkle with ¼ cup of the bread crumbs and stir them in. You should be able to make a crab cake that just holds together but is still a bit wet. If the mixture is too wet to hold together (and it might be, depending on how wet the crab and cooked rice are), stir in up to ¼ cup more bread crumbs.

2. Form the mixture into eight 1-inch-thick cakes and put on a plate or platter. Refrigerate for 1 hour to firm them up.

3. When ready to cook the crab cakes, heat ½ inch oil in a large nonstick skillet and preheat the oven to 250°F. Spread about 1 cup bread crumbs on a plate and lightly dredge the crab cakes in bread crumbs. Fry the crab cakes in 2 batches until golden on both sides and heated through, 3 to 4 minutes per side. Drain the first batch on paper towels and keep them warm in the oven while you cook the second batch. Season the crab cakes with salt and serve with lemon wedges.

MAGNIFICENT MEATBALLS

Makes **about 2 dozen medium meatballs, depending on which family raised you!**

1 large onion, cut into chunks

3 garlic cloves

1 pound ground pork

1 pound ground veal

2 large eggs

½ cup freshly grated
Parmigiano-Reggiano,
plus more for serving

½ cup freshly grated Pecorino
Romano

1½ cups unseasoned fresh
bread crumbs

¼ cup chopped fresh
Italian parsley

Pinch of crushed red
pepper flakes

Kosher salt and freshly
ground black pepper

Canola and olive oil,
for frying

**EDITOR'S
WINE CHOICE**
Earthy, slightly
herbal Chianti
Classico.

*Here bread crumbs and pureed onions magically act to bind the
proteins and keep the meat moist and almost creamy. Although
undetectable in the end result, these tricks will serve you well.*

1. In a food processor, combine the onion, garlic, and 1 cup water. Puree
until very smooth. In a large mixing bowl, combine the pork, veal, eggs,
Parmigiano-Reggiano, Pecorino Romano, bread crumbs, parsley, pepper
flakes, and salt and pepper. Add the onion puree and, with your hands,
mix until *just* combined. Form 1 small meatball and fry, just to taste for
seasoning, and adjust if necessary.

2. Wet your hands and form the meat mixture into 24 meatballs. Don't
overwork the mixture—the meatballs should be light and soft, not spongy
and tough. Put the meatballs on a rimmed sheet pan and refrigerate
30 minutes to firm them up.

3. Preheat the oven to 350°F. When ready to fry, in a large skillet over
medium heat, heat enough canola and olive oil (equal amounts of each)
to come one third of the way up the sides of the meatballs. Fry the
meatballs, in batches, until browned all over, about 6 minutes per batch.
Drain and place on a rimmed sheet pan. When all the meatballs are
browned, place in the oven and bake until cooked through, about
15 minutes. (The browned meatballs can also be finished by simmering
in marinara or another tomato sauce for 30 minutes.) Serve with
heaps of finely shredded Parmigiano-Reggiano.

FRENCH TOAST WITH EARL GREY SYRUP

Serves **4**

EARL GREY SYRUP

- **1 cup sugar**
- **4 Earl Grey tea bags**

FRENCH TOAST

- **4 large eggs**
- **¾ cup whole milk**
- **¾ cup heavy cream**
- **2 tablespoons sugar**
- **1 teaspoon pure vanilla extract**
- **Pinch of kosher salt**
- **2 tablespoons (¼ stick) unsalted butter, plus more for serving**
- **Eight 1-inch-thick slices challah bread or good-quality white bread**

When I created this special syrup, I had been trying to come up with an interesting and unique brunch condiment. I then simply steeped Earl Grey tea in a one-to-one sugar and water solution, and the end result tasted fantastic paired with French toast. This easy syrup can be made ahead and rewarmed in a small saucepan or in the microwave when ready to serve. Any leftover syrup can be used to sweeten hot tea or stored in the refrigerator for later use.

1. To make the syrup In a small saucepan, bring 1 cup water to a boil. Add the sugar and simmer until the sugar is dissolved. Remove from the heat, add the tea bags, and let steep 5 minutes. Discard the tea bags. Bring the sweetened tea to a rapid simmer and cook until syrupy (about the thickness of real maple syrup), 6 to 7 minutes. You should have about ¾ cup syrup.

2. To make the French toast Preheat the oven to 250°F. In a large bowl, whisk together the eggs, milk, cream, sugar, vanilla, and salt. In a large nonstick skillet, melt 1 tablespoon of the butter over medium heat. Submerge 4 slices of the bread in the egg mixture and let soak about 30 seconds, turning to make sure the slices are evenly soaked. Let the excess egg mixture drip back into the bowl.

3. Cook the bread in the butter until golden on both sides, 2 to 3 minutes per side. Keep the first batch warm in the oven while you make the second batch with the remaining 1 tablespoon butter and the last 4 slices of bread. Serve the French toast warm with additional butter and drizzle with the warm Earl Grey syrup.

WHITE GAZPACHO

Total **15 min plus 1 hr chilling**; Serves **4**

- 10 ounces hothouse cucumber, peeled and sliced (about 2 cups)
- 1 cup green grapes
- ½ cup marcona almonds
- ½ cup coarsely chopped fennel
- ¼ cup white verjus (see Note)
- 2 tablespoons sherry vinegar
- 1 tablespoon honey
- 1 cup extra-virgin olive oil
- Kosher salt

"I've always loved toying with different vegetables and vinegars in gazpacho recipes," Geoffrey Zakarian says. *For his take on tomato-less white gazpacho, he blends fennel and buttery marcona almonds with the usual grapes and cucumbers. Verjus, the juice from unripened wine grapes, gives the chilled soup tanginess without the puckery jolt of harsher vinegars.*

In a blender, combine the cucumber, grapes, almonds, fennel, verjus, vinegar and honey. Puree until very smooth, about 30 seconds. With the blender on, slowly drizzle in the olive oil. Season with salt. Pass the soup through a fine strainer, if desired. Refrigerate until well chilled, about 1 hour, before serving.

NOTE Verjus, the tart juice pressed from unripe grapes, is available at specialty food stores.

FOR MORE ON GEOFFREY ZAKARIAN

geoffreyzakarian.com

🅕 Geoffrey Zakarian

🐦 @gzchef

CREDITS

AMERICA—FARM TO TABLE
Excerpted from the book *America–Farm to Table* by Mario Batali and Jim Webster. Copyright © 2014 by Mario Batali LLC. Reprinted by permission of Grand Central Publishing, New York, NY. All rights reserved. Recipe photography by Quentin Bacon. Photograph of Mario Batali on p. 12 of *Best of the Best* copyright © 2014 by Kelly Campbell.

A GOOD FOOD DAY
"Escarole Salad with Pear and Pecorino," "Cream-Free Creamed Corn," and "Braised Chicken Thighs with Garlic, Lemon, and Greek Olives" from *A Good Food Day: Reboot Your Health with Food That Tastes Great* by Marco Canora with Tammy Walker, foreword by Tim Ferriss, copyright © 2014 by Marco Canora. Used by permission of Clarkson Potter/Publishers, an imprint of the Crown Publishing Group, a division of Penguin Random House LLC. All rights reserved. Photographs copyright © 2014 by Michael Harlan Turkell.

TACOLICIOUS
Photographs, by Alex Farnum, photographs copyright © 2014 by Alex Farnum; "Melon, Mango, and Cucumber with Chile, Salt, and Lime," "Carnitas Taco," and "Lone Star Breakfast Taco" from *Tacolicious: Festive Recipes for Tacos, Snacks, Cocktails, and More* by Sara Deseran with Joe Hargrave, Antelmo Faria, and Mike Barrow, copyright © 2014 by Sara Deseran and Joe Hargrave. Used by permission of Ten Speed Press, an imprint of the Crown Publishing Group, a division of Penguin Random House LLC. All rights reserved.

SMASHING PLATES
From *Smashing Plates: Greek Flavors Redefined* by Maria Elia. Text copyright © 2013 Maria Elia. Photography copyright © 2013 Jenny Zarins. Used by permission of Kyle Books.

INSIDE THE TEST KITCHEN
Photographs, "Caesar Dressing," "Spaghetti with Summer Squash and Pine Nuts," and "Herb-Roasted Wild Mushrooms with Red Wine and Cream" from *Inside the Test Kitchen: 120 New Recipes, Perfected* by Tyler Florence, text and photographs copyright © 2014 by Tyler Florence. Used by permission of Clarkson Potter/Publishers, an imprint of the Crown Publishing Group, a division of Penguin Random House LLC. All rights reserved.

THE KITCHN COOKBOOK
Photographs, "Skillet-Roasted Whole Chicken," "Pasta Casserole with Broccoli and Gouda Cheese," and "Roasted Eggplant with Smoked Almonds and Goat Cheese" from *The Kitchn Cookbook: Recipes, Kitchens & Tips to Inspire Your Cooking* by Sara Kate Gillingham, copyright © 2014 by Apartment Therapy LLC. Used by permission of Clarkson Potter/Publishers, an imprint of the Crown Publishing Group, a division of Penguin Random House LLC. All rights reserved. Photographs by Leela Cyd.

CARLA'S COMFORT FOODS
From *Carla's Comfort Foods: Favorite Dishes from Around the World* by Carla Hall with Genevieve Ko. Copyright © 2014 by Carla Hall. Photographs copyright © 2014 by Frances Janisch. Used by permission of Atria Books.

PRUNE
Photographs, by Eric Wolfinger, copyright © 2014 by Eric Wolfinger; "Avocado Sandwich with Lemon Ricotta," "Salt-Packed Cold Roast Beef with Bread Crumb Salsa," and "Grilled Lamb Blade Chops" from *Prune* by Gabrielle Hamilton, copyright © 2014 by Gabrielle Hamilton. Used by permission of Random House, an imprint and division of Penguin Random House LLC. All rights reserved.

VIBRANT FOOD
Photographs, "Apricot and Chicken Salad with Toasted Cumin Vinaigrette," "Smoky Red Pepper Soup with Pumpkin Seeds and Feta," and "Chile-Roasted Delicata Squash with Queso Fresco" from *Vibrant Food: Celebrating the Ingredients, Recipes, and Colors of Each Season* by Kimberley Hasselbrink, text and photography copyright © 2014 by Kimberley Hasselbrink. Used by permission of Ten Speed Press, an imprint of the Crown Publishing Group, a division of Penguin Random House LLC. All rights reserved.

A CHANGE OF APPETITE
From *A Change of Appetite: Where Healthy Meets Delicious* by Diana Henry. Text copyright © Diana Henry 2014. Photography copyright © Laura Edwards 2014. Used by permission of Mitchell Beazley.

BROWN SUGAR KITCHEN
From *Brown Sugar Kitchen* © 2014 by Tanya Holland; with photographs by Jody Horton. Used with permission of Chronicle Books LLC, San Francisco. Visit ChronicleBooks.com

FOOD&WINE
BOOKS

More books from
FOOD&WINE

Annual Cookbook
More than 650 recipes from the world's best cooks, including culinary legends Jacques Pépin and Alice Waters as well as star chefs like Bobby Flay, Alex Guarnaschelli and Giada De Laurentiis.

Cocktails
Over 150 new and classic recipes from America's most brilliant bartenders. Plus an indispensable guide to cocktail basics and the top new bars and lounges around the country.

Wine Guide
An essential, pocket-size guide focusing on the world's most reliable producers, with over 1,000 stellar wines.

**TO ORDER, CALL 800-284-4145
OR VISIT FOODANDWINE.COM/BOOKS**